A
ROAD TRANSPORT
HERITAGE

BOB TUCK

Published by Bob Tuck
Low Worsall, Yarm,
Cleveland England TS15 9QA

ISBN 0 9521938 0 9

First Published 1993

Other books by Bob Tuck

Moving Mountains
Mountain Movers
Mammoth Trucks
Hauling Heavyweights
The Supertrucks of Scammell
Move It (compendium of *Moving Mountains*
and *Mountain Movers*)
Carrying Cargo
Classic Hauliers
Robsons
Classic Hauliers 2
The Golden Days Of Heavy Haulage

Printed in Great Britain by
The Amadeus Press Ltd
Huddersfield, West Yorkshire.

Typesetting by Highlight Type Bureau Ltd
Shipley, West Yorkshire.

CONTENTS

Front cover - Spiers of Melksham.

Established in 1896, The Warminster Motor Company may not come readily to mind in the archives of road transport but since 1952 it's been the concern behind the famous name of Spiers of Melksham. Bill Spiers bought up The Warminster Group of garages after the Spiers fleet had been nationalised. It wasn't long however before Bill got back into wagons and his trademark was soon to become these brown, red and white AEC Mandators. Always buying second hand, Spiers sourced their AEC purchases from all over the UK although the Amoco Oil Company was one well remembered supplier. OYO 140R was one of a batch of ten falling in the group OYO 136R - 152R which were bought ex Amoco during 1982. The 2TG4R tractor unit was chassis number 34041 it being dated from 1976 and like most of Spiers AECs, was powered by the AV760 engine. It's not surprising that Spiers - like a few others - mourned the passing of the Mandator although Bill's son William Spiers now favours similar coloured second hand ERFs for artic traction.

Back cover - Hills of Botley.

June 1964 found TOT 297 about to leave Fratton goods yard at Portsmouth, this 45 ton concrete beam being destined for the Havant by pass. The Scammell Explorer with Jack Collins driving and Brian Vear as mate was one of five Hill vehicles involved in this Anglia Concrete job. The 6x6 Constructor 358 ETN driven by Titch Notley can be seen at the rear whilst also involved were 874 AUU - the 6x4 Junior Constructor driven by Jim Purvis - 298 FUW - a 4x4 Mountaineer with Brian Mathews driving and MUH 21 - a Pioneer with Jack Murphy driving. Carrying this beam is a 65 ton capacity Eagle low loader which is running on four axles of four in line 14.00x20 tyres. Due to it's design, the entire weight of the beam had to be supported centrally.

Front and back end papers

Having been born and bred at Delves Lane, which is just outside Consett in County Durham, my impressionable early years were dominated by the vehicles that came in and out of Consett Iron Company. Like most big works, the focal point for a lorry enthusiast was the weighbridge and although I was obviously trespassing, those unknown weighmen always seemed to turn a blind eye to that schoolboy on his bike. Like many who look back with a tinge of regret, I wish I had photographed more of those long distance vehicles who had made the trek to Consett. It was to be financial constraints - pocket money - that dictated how often I could visit Boots to purchase and process films. The technique and quality of what I recorded doesn't match the many professionals who are featured throughout this book but to those like me that followed transport in Consett, the contents at least give an emotional slice of what passed through the town during the late 1950s.

Title Page - K.Fell & Co

It was to be their localised form of operations which saved the long established Westmoreland concern of K Fell & Co from compulsory nationalisation. However within a couple of years of this 1950 tidal wave, Kirby Fell had sold the business to Captain AB Davy who was perhaps better known locally for his coal factoring interests. The new company owner is pictured on the far left leaning against his Austin Sheerline motor car. The Perkins engined Seddons were used on milk churn collection work, the two on the far left being registered HTF 759 and JM 5711 whilst the sole ERF is HTF 773. The quartet of Ford Thames tippers were used to haul stone out of the local Whitbarrow quarry. Because this site couldn't be blasted, the quarrymen used to throw stones up at the rock face to create avalanches and bring the stone tumbling down to ground level prior to loading. Fells were to diversify into general haulage during the 1950s and moved from Grange to a purpose built site next to the Libby factory at Milnthorpe in 1957. The business and premises were to be taken over by Bewick Transport Services in 1976.

ACKNOWLEDGEMENTS

Once again, I owe a great deal of thanks to the many people who have given me the time and consideration needed to prepare a book of this nature. Those specifically helping with photographs were : Ken Archer, Derek Bailey, Mick Bradley, Allan & Anne Burnes, Alastair Carter, Dennis Charles, Brian Cowburn, Arthur Duckett, Joe Elliott, Alan Ferguson, Ben Ford, John Foster, Dick Franklin, Alec Hewitt, Jack Hill, Alan Hopps, Anthony Hotham, Ian Manship, Peter Midgley, Eric Morton, Howard Nunnick, John Pattinson, Mark Richards, Stuart Ritchie, Gerald Rooke, Bryan Salkeld, Frank Scaife, Dennis Smith, William Spiers, Mick Swain, Chris Swindlehirst, Stewart Ward, Paul Wardle, Keith Watkinson, Tim Wayne, Jim Wilkinson, Ralph Willmott, Robert Willson, Colin Wilson and John Wynn.

Taking the time to trawl the memory banks and record books for nuggets of information were : Ronnie Atkinson, Robbie and Alex Boyes, Philip Braithwaite, Peter Clemmett, George Curtis, Joe Devey, Bert Eastwood, Derek Freeland, Tony Graves, Alan Martin, Jackie Milburn, John Mollett, Jeff Newton, Steve Phillips, Dennis Robinson, Albert Smith, Eric Steel, Henry Stocks, Walter Tomlinson and David Waterhouse.

I would never forget Roger and Betty Kenny who continue to afford unselfish help in what's really for them not the best of times. Last but never least, many thanks to my wife Sylvia - E Ferro Ferrum Temperatum - twelve down, twelve more to go?

AUTHOR'S PREFACE

Modern day road transport is a demanding service industry. The priority is always today's and tomorrow's work so as long as yesterday's load is paid for, then it's quickly forgotten.

In such an atmosphere, it is easy to gloss over the past and leave nostalgia for those with ample spare time on their hands. However, the history of road transport is one that shouldn't be simply dismissed in this fashion, because like any quickly evolving industry it relies on it's solid roots in order to establish exciting growth for the future.

In this volume I once again look back into the archives of road haulage. Being aware that a photograph is worth a thousand words, my text has been curtailed to indepth captions. In touching on the background to more than 40 different transport concerns, I know I am hardly scratching the surface of the heritage to the industry - even though all those covered in the book have made their contribution to it's history.

Bob Tuck.

Percy William Archer began his link with the motor industry in 1920 when he opened up Station Garage in South Parade, Northallerton. His first wagons were involved in emptying dustbins although OMH 190 dates from 1947, the Ford based outfit being bought ex Army. Originally built to carry sections of pre-fabricated buildings, Archers shortend the semi-trailer to make it more practical for either hauling furniture carrying containers or as pictured, tractor carriage. Seen in East Road, Northallerton the outfit is carrying about two tons in the Massey Harrison 102 Twin Power Junior and Allis Chalmers tractors that have been in for repair. This Ford together with DLG 369, an ERF artic, were the two Archer outfits compulsorily acquired when nationalisation came to Northallerton in 1950.

Removals were specifically exempted from nationalisation and it was to be this 1950s quartet which maintained Archer's link with the haulage world. Between the two Bedfords CVN 38 and HRK 282 is LUB 343, a diesel powered Albion which started life with Leeds based 'Burton the Tailor' and was regularly driven at Archers by Ernie Hope. The Guy Vixen on the far left is EPY 20 which was collected new from the Wolverhampton factory by George Woodburn on November 25, 1947, it being supplied through the Leeds dealership of Wheatley & Whiteley. George drove north bearing the trade plates 025 AJ, it being February 1948 before the vehicle was bodied and licensed for road work. Gilbert Alderson was the regular driver of the Guy which is recalled as loosing it's radiator mounted Indian head, mid way up Wass bank enroute for Scarborough. This vehicle ended it's days as a standing store at the Northallerton motor dealership of Kellett & Pick.

On June 5, 1959, as a means of expansion, Archers were to buy out the long established Ripon concern of Richard Thorpe Ltd. Although originating from the turn of the century, Thorpe's were not to go limited until November 1,1944, when the named directors were given then as Mary Ann Thorpe, Edward Thorpe and Edna May Thorpe. Edward - or Ted as he was known - was founder Richard Thorpe's son and is seen in 1915 at their Ripon base with a full load of kit bags. M2209 was a Foden 5 tonner being works number 1848 and new to Thorpe in 1909. Ted Thorpe was to see war time service and it's not surprising that some of that time was spent driving big traction engines in France.

When Archers bought the Thorpe concern, the road fleet was then made up of two vehicles - a K series Austin and a petrol engined Thornycroft plus the carrier's licence for a spare vehicle. GWY 155 stayed in service for some time even though it's recalled as having a 'back to front' gear change pattern. The Austin soon made way for 746 AAJ, a four cylinder engined TK Bedford which was chassis number 151790. The spare licence was put onto this VW, 7178 UA, which was used for jobs up to about a ton in weight until it was blown off the road at Catterick one day in 1967. In 1964 the Thornycroft went to auction and was replaced in service by a TK Bedford artic. Archers continued to operate the Thorpe concern as a seperate entity until the Ripon business was closed in 1970.

As Percy Archer spent most of his time in the High Street shop, the transport interests were looked after by his son John - or Brenny as he was usually known. A big fan of the Albion marque, XVN 48 was to be his flagship when it came into service in 1960. The Caladonian was a type 24C1 being chassis number 57234B. Equipped with a Leyland 600 engine and double drive bogie, regular driver Alfie Grange was normally engaged carrying bagged fertiliser from Fisons plant at Goole for storage by Archers at Spring Well Lane. This fine looking eight wheeler was a casualty of the Archer fleet contraction and was laid up in 1968. It was sold about 1970, when loaded up with an Albion Reiver and a four wheeled Albion Victor - CAJ 681C - in triple deck fashion, it was driven to the Coates scrapyard in Newcastle to an unknown fate.

By the early 1960s, the Northallerton removal fleet had expanded both in numbers and size. LTP 269 was a 5.1 litre engined Austin dating from 1955, the second hand vehicle being bought in Southampton although at the time was fitted with a brand new body. XPY 174 was a 1960 Albion Chieftan being chassis number 75256K. It cost Archers £2,245 when new and had an unladen weight of 4ton 11cwt. Very much second hand was FSC 408 which dates from 1947 and was bought specifically by Archers for it's carriers licence. The main difference to the two TJ Bedfords was that TPY 680 was fitted with twin rear wheels whilst VAJ 601 only had singles. The latter was the pride and joy of driver Tommy Preston who always seemed to have a polishing cloth in his hand. As the backdrop suggests, Percy Archer had diversified into a furniture shop and auction room on a prime site in Northallerton's High Street.

The general haulage vehicles of Archers are pictured one Sunday morning during March 1962. Next to the eight wheeled Caladonian on the far left, is a six wheeled double drive Albion Reiver. UVN 947 wasn't destined to last however, although after being written off in an accident, was replaced by an identical Reiver chassis number 67277C that was registered AAJ 760B. Having the 300 engine and Eaton two speed axle, UPY 398 was a long wheelbase 'S' type Bedford that had John Dunning as it's regular driver and although fitted with tipping gear was normally used, like the Atkinson beside it, on Hotpoint traffic. The washing machine manufacturer had a distribution point at Brompton - just outside Northallerton - and Jack Cook driving PWT 314 normally hauled 15-20 drops for delivery to shops in the Glasgow/Edinburgh area. The 5LW powered Atky was model L745(E) being chassis number FC4012 and fitted with the 557CM gearbox. Bought second hand at Leeds, the flat bodied vehicle sports a concertina style of canvas tilt that cut load covering time down to a minimum. After it's days at Archers, the Atkinson passed onto the showground circuit.

Recalled for their resplendent yellow livery, Edward Beck had originally been in business as a building contractor so it's under-standable that his first heavy haulage outfits ran under the banner of Contractor's (Transport) Ltd. The name was soon to be dropped in favour of the Edward Beck title but OJA 351 - one of three similar TS3s - sports both the Beck company names. The two stroke powered Commer dates from 1959 and is pictured in Altrincham loaded with gas pipes. Jimmy Peters is stood beside the tractor which had air over hydraulic brakes and was good for loads up to 10 ton.

KDB 703 dates from 1955 and came to Becks second hand. Pictured at Salford docks, it's one of two Beck outfits loading a Caterpillar grader - ex USA - for delivery to Cannock. Graham Phillips was the outfit's mate on this job, the driver Danny being stood on the neck of the Dyson step frame semi-trailer. When finished at Becks, it's believed the Gardner powered Foden went for export.

As the fleet number proudly proclaims, YJA 186 was the first of three mobile cranes ran by Becks and dates from 1963. The Hydrocon mechanism had a folding jib to it, the vehicle being regularly driven by Len Everington. It's pictured in Wharton Cranes on Station Road, Reddish rigging up an overhead crane prior to testing. Edward Beck was to retire about 1970 and the business based in Greg Street, Reddish, Stockport was closed down prior to him moving to the Isle of Man.

Who'd be a heavy haulage driver in conditions like this? YCY 221 is carrying a 15 ton pressure tank section that had been made by Joseph Adamson and is seen easing it's way through Hyde. Negotiating trolley bus wires is now mainly a thing of the past but in the 1960s most corporations who ran this mode of public transport also had something like this converted Bedford bus as a wire lifter. Dave Osborne was the driver's mate for this load which was running about 18' high. Pictured at the rear is KDB 703 which was running in ballasted form to assist on the many tricky parts of the move.

Currently running an eighty strong fleet under the banner of Bewick Transport Services Ltd from Milnthorpe in Cumbria, Dennis Smith traces his haulage roots back to the 19th century. On the other side of the Penines, his great grandfather Thomas Bewick had established himself on a dedicated carrier route between Consett and Newcastle. First with horses and carts, on the arrival of steam Bewicks were to adapt to the well liked Fodens. The driver - who was known as Black Jack - is pictured at the wheel of 'Excelsior' which was new in May 1911. The vehicle bore the maker's number 2562 and was sold in 1915.

John Wilson, Stanley Dunning and Wilfred Barker created the company of Bee Line Safety Coaches in 1934. Starting with four brand new Dennis Lancet coaches, the partners expanded into road haulage during 1936 from their base on Stockton Road at West Hartlepool. The company expanded by buying up licences and vehicles from other operators notably the 14 strong fleet of Lamberts from Billingham in 1944. Bee Line were to specialise in a London trunk with about six wagons leaving West every weekday around 6.30pm. In the main these eight wheelers were loaded with the produce of the Cerebos factory at Greatham being delivered to their main depot at Willesden. Colin Wilson - John's son - took this photograph of the Burn Road depot at Christmas 1948 which illustrates how the fleet had become dominated by AEC Mammoth Majors. In 1949 the entire fleet of 25 were compulsorily acquired by BRS with the Diamond T wrecker - pictured at the top of the line - soon moved to BRS Thornaby. Bee Line Coaches were to peak around the 60 mark and were sold to the Ellerman Group in the 1970s.

Pictured with his son John, Thomas Bewick is seen outside Woodside House, Westwood on what's known locally as the Low Road at Ebchester. M 5527 was new in September 1913 having maker's number 3992. The vehicle bore the name of 'Dorothy' and was sold in 1917. Bewick was to expand his fleet to about seven, the demountable bodied Fodens travelling as far afield as Southampton and Scotland. This photograph was actually a postcard sent from a potential customer - Clarke Bros of 67, Cutler's Hall Road, Blackhill. The words on the card read "Dear Sir, We can do with you for one day this week. Can you come tomorrow - Wednesday." With the card being franked 12.30pm Tuesday 23rd February, it's apparent that an old penny stamp was enough to keep the wheels of industry turning in pre-telephone days. Thomas did intend passing the business onto his son but sadly John returned from the 1914-18 war suffering badly from the effects of a gas attack. Bewick senior thus sold his well established business to the local railway operators about 1921.

Bewick's first artic was to be a modestly powered Leyland Mastiff but Dennis Smith - seen in the centre with his brother Richard on the right - soon turned to the Atkinson Borderer as his favoured traction. Driver Derek Chambers - who is now the company transport manager - was given both 98K then 480L when they came new into service. Supplied by Scotts of Penrith with 220 Cummins engines, the Atkys ran in the main to the Home Counties carrying paper from Henry Cooke's. Back loads from the south east were normally paper sacks delivered into Lancashire. OJM 480L was recalled as having a phenomenal motorway performance although first ratios in it's Eaton two speed axle meant top gear was too high to engage. 260 and 98K were later sold to Leyland Paints who ran them on for extended service.

Opposite above: Dixies Garage at Sandside, Milnthorpe has been the base for Hudson's diverse operations for as long as anyone can remember. J.B.Hudson started with a horse and cart but it was his daughter, Maggie Bowman, who really became the concern's driving force. Starting up again after nationalisation, Maggie was running about six Leyland Octopus eight wheelers when she died in 1960. This road fleet was sold first to Athersmiths but when the Licensing Authority declined a transfer request to move the carrier licences to their base at Barrow, Athersmiths sold the fleet on again to K.Fell & Co about 1967. In turn Fells were to be taken over by Bewick Transport Services in 1976. This Chris Swindlehirst photograph dates from about 1947 and shows two of Hudsons Leylands at work at Morecambe football ground. EO 5073 - believed to be a Lynx - is facing a 6x4 Hippo with Randolph Sewell stood on the left. With him is Arthur Fazackly who was eventually to give up wagon driving to set up his own driving school.

Opposite below: After cutting his teeth on a Thames Trader, Dennis Smith invested £3,600 in this Ford D Series 1000, bought new through Skippers of Kendal. Then aged 21, Smith had decided to resurrect the use of his great grandfather's Bewick name as a trading title to distinguish himself from all the other Smiths then in transport. FJM 400F was powered by a Cummins V8 180 engine and is seen at Staveley loaded with 10 tons of tomato ketchup. Smith's early traffic regularly took him to London and the South East whilst accompanying him virtually every where he went was his whippet Judy.

The uncompromising strength of the Scammell is epitomised in this solid tyred Edward Box 45 tonner seen at the Davey United Darnall works in Sheffield during 1939 supporting a press destined for Russia. Leaning against the cab is the Manchester based driver Jock Cruickshank who had just joined Box after leaving Pickfords. The smart figure at the rear of the outfit is Eric Morton who was then engaged on shunting duties for Box's at Sheffield. After helping Jock load, it was Eric's job to chauffeur the Corporation Highway's man - Mr Day - along behind the load as it was escorted through the town by either P.C.s Lloyd or 'Ginger' Bailey. Mr Day's job was to make a note of any damage the loaded outfit caused to the highway prior to sending the bill for repair to Box.

Opposite below: No discourse on transport heritage would be complete without reference to KD 9168, Scammell's first 100 tonner built for Marston Road Services Ltd. A change in name to Edward Box - but no change in ownership - highlighted the fierce competition during the 1930s with Norman E.Box. No dispute in the vehicle's strength however, as it hauls a 98 ton locomotive along the East Lancs Road from the Vulcan foundry at Newton-le-Willows to Liverpool's Gladstone dock during 1938. Tommy Wolstenholme is driving, Dave Warbrooke the mate and Eric Penquet the steersman whilst George Bramall is driving the ex Newcastle Electric Co Scammell giving him a pull to save a gear or two on the undulating road. The big Scammell sports it's modified fuel tank of 200 gallon capacity fitted by Box to the roof which then gravity fed the Scammell's dashboard mounted scuttle tank. Stopped one day at a cafe in Conisborough, the mate forgot to turn the tap off and the overflow of diesel soaked the Scammell's clutch. No panic for the crew who simply put Fullers Earth into the mechanism to re-instate it's operation.

In their heyday during the mid 1950s, the Distington Engineering reputation for ingot mould production was second to none. With exports going to Canada, Holland, Germany and Sweden, it wasn't unusual to see such a line up waiting to leave the Chapelbank works. SUA 710 was chassis number 35948 and new to the Park Group depot in Sheffield's Stainforth Road on December 18, 1953, when it was given the fleet number 63D268. KKW 3, with Foden two stroke engine, was chassis number 36674 and had the fleet number 32D333 being based first at Bradford before being transferred to Leeds in 1956. Both the Fodens were to give BRS another 10 years of service. Checking the mould's paper work are security men Jack Fearon and Archie Rose. Heaviest load is the 15 ton mould being carried by the A.M.Walker Atkinson which is fourth in line. Whilst the garden and tennis court have gone to make way for a bus rank and car park, the bowling green still exists. The three managerial figures stood in front of it being Joe Dixon, Rupert Lancaster and Reggy Yates.

Opposite: It was the newly elected Labour Government's mandate of 1945 that was to create the nationalised road haulage operation of British Road Services although in practice it didn't really start up until about three years later. All manner of vehicles were compulsorily and voluntarily acquired into government ownership and then moved round the country to various BRS depots. JEH 578 dates from 1944, the Bedford starting life at Stoke-on-Trent. It was one of a handful that were relocated to Preston, the Scammell semi-automatic trailer couplings being well liked for the Irish ferry work. Seen in the Distington plant at Workington about 1952, there's less than seven tons in this storage tank made by the Central Engineering workshops and bound for sunnier climes.

9H50 sports general trade plates number 973 TW and was the Bishop's Stortford wrecker although prior to nationalisation had been ran by Eastern Roadways. This haulier had bought the ex War Department Ward le France from a surplus sale at St Albans in 1947. Mick Bradley was workshops foreman at the time and recalled going to collect the vehicle. Before he left St Albans, Mick had spent two days rummaging through wooden boxes for a suitable worm gear to get the p.t.o. driven winch working correctly. The petrol driven six wheeler was recalled as having a dual circuit ignition with both coil and magneto linked to the two sparking plugs per cylinder. The wrecker was still in service in 1956 when Mick left the depot but the fate of the vehicle after that is unknown.

Although Scunthorpe depot ran overnight trunk vehicles to Whitehaven, driver Gordon Hall - or Blossom as he was nicknamed due to his waggoner past - worked a roaming itinerary. Distington Engineering really liked to see him as his was the only eight wheeled rigid the company'd encountered which could safely handle these 17.5 ton slag ladles that were destined for the Appleby-Frodingham works in Scunthorpe. Gordon reckoned his Leyland Octopus was slightly over tyred and was thus able to handle this weight although the rigid was still a handful to hold in check when descending the likes of Galley Bank on the A66 near Bowes. The Octopus only had vacuum-hydraulic brakes it being chassis number 501638 and new to BRS on October 16, 1950. It worked at Scunthorpe until it was sold on November 22, 1962.

Tommy Giles, the regular driver of MXB 215, is pictured in this Ben Ford photograph at rest at the bottom of Marlborough Hill on the A4 in Wiltshire during 1958. His five cylinder Gardner engined ERF was chassis number 6095 and new to BRS in 1952 it coming to the Hayes & Slough branch in 1955. Together with sister four wheeler 1A412, this vehicle regularly carried 40' long loads by resting them on the trestle support to take them over the cab. Tommy's outward load had been a crane jib from Ardecar Ltd at Kings Cross, London although hidden beneath the sheets is his modest back load from Bristol. Originally numbered 46A486, the ERF was sold by BRS on June 12, 1961.

Driver Clements is seen on the A30 at Bagshot in Surrey during 1958 with quite a long haul ahead of him. The 14 tons of steel reinforcing bars were to be taken from the National Gas Turbine Establishment at Pyestock near Farnborough, up to the new Spadeadam rocket site being built on the Northumberland/Cumberland border. Having the Foden two stroke engine, chassis number 30096 was new to BRS on February 1, 1950. Originally allocated to Bermondsey, it first had the fleet number 6A20. When transferred to Hayes in 1955 it became first 46A508, then renumbered 1A4018 in October 1956 then 1A418 in February 1957. It was sold by BRS on April 10, 1961.

Reg Darbin is pictured in 1959 having just pulled into May's transport cafe, his load of railway sleepers being enroute from RAF Wethersfield in Essex to George Wimpey's depot at Southall. The Guy Otter is recalled as having a Moss gearbox which had it's shift pattern the 'wrong way round' to that normally followed with the lower gears being closest to the driver. Chassis number ODTP45064 was new to BRS on December 1, 1953, it being allocated to Hayes & Slough during 1955. It too received several fleet numbers in the BRS re-organisations but in April 1961 it was transferred to East Anglia district and given the number 3A468. The Guy was sold by BRS on October 1, 1962.

Although the Hayes branch of BRS was responsible for quite a lot of long load work, it was really traffic inherited via the nationalised concern of H.Burgoynes from Westferry Road, Millwall. Whilst MLF 277 was new to BRS on December 1, 1951, the single axle bogie was one that had been home made by Burgoynes. There's about 20 tons in this load of 50' long steel piles destined for Demolition & Construction Ltd, Mitcham Road, Croydon. Regular driver of this outfit was 'Busby' Jackson who, because he was one of six brothers - four of whom worked for BRS - was known as Jackson 4. The Leyland Octopus was chassis number 514615, it being sold by BRS on April 9, 1962.

MLE 20 was new to BRS on September 1, 1951, the Leyland Octopus being a model 22.0/1 and chassis number 512645. First seeing service at Bermondsey, the eight wheeler went to the West London Group, then Islington before going to Hayes in 1956. Pictured in 1958, driver Frank Laurie - on the left of the two figures - is unloading the 13 tons of steel girders at the J.H.Sankey factory at Wellington in Shropshire. The steel had come from T.C.Jones of Wood Lane, London. Jones were part of the George Cohen Group who in turn were at the time the selling agency for Jones Cranes - no connection to T.C.Jones - and understandably the crane in shot is of Jones manufacture. BRS were to sell this Leyland on April 9, 1962.

Four smiling faces seen on the A2 Rochester Way in Kent but it had been a wasted journey in late 1959 for these Hayes outfits as they'd gone to the Isle of Grain hoping to collect some 40' pipes. Right to left the figures are Lofty Hughes - the driver of OLB 96 - Reg Harbin - the driver of OLB 35, the Guy artic at the rear - George Pearson, driver of NUC 971 and his mate Harry Jarrett. The Octopus was chassis number 530806 and new to BRS on June 1, 1953, but once again it's drawing a rather special Burgoynes trailer. The Seddon tractor unit was chassis number 8936 and new to BRS South West London Group at Battersea. It was transferred to Tufnell Park in 1956 before going to Hayes in 1959. The Seddon was sold by BRS on June 12, 1961 whilst the Leyland was ran until August 12, 1963, before it's sale.

Ben Ford found KYK 772 unloading this ventilation plant at Northfleet power station in 1959, the load having come from Air Control Installations Ltd, Victoria Road, West Ruislip. The Leyland Octopus was chassis number 501167 and new to BRS on May 23, 1950, it going first to Islington before transfer to Hayes in 1956. Regular driver here was Tom Lewis who used the normal truck sheet trick of partially blanking off the radiator to generate a bit more heat. The eight wheeler was sold by BRS on June 19, 1961.

Modern day long load carriers would look at this combination and say it just shouldn't work. Although there was a turntable mounted on the back of the Leyland Octopus, the 50' Shepley made chimney is chained directly onto the trailer. The only turning movement thus allowed for the load is that which is transmitted through the trailer drawbar as it follows the drawing vehicle. Loads, thus, had to be made strong to withstand such carriage. SNF 951 was based at Wentworth Street, Ardwick in Manchester for all it's life. The Leyland Octopus was chassis number 552322, first registered on February 8, 1956, and ran by BRS until early 1965.

Perhaps it was a flashback to the famous eight wheeled Showboat vans ran by Fisher Renwicks in pre-nationalisation days, but BRS Parcels made great use of the eight wheeler during the 1950s before finally opting for articulation. Just as distinctive as their red liveried brethren, the green parcel vans ran their own long distance routes with Ben Ford spotting 33A431 a long way from home. NXP 223 was chassis number 3871.1239 and new to the Metropolitan Parcels Group in 1953. It worked all it's life at the Muswell Hill depot in Coppett's Road but on April 5, 1958, it was found bracing the elements at Scotch Corner. The AEC Mammoth Major was renumbered P40A74 as part of the North West London Parcels Group and sold on July 22, 1963.

NVP 98 was in the first phase of 200 vehicles built by Bristol for BRS it being chassis number 88.135 when first registered on February 1, 1954. The eight wheeler went to the North Nottingham Group as fleet number 63E282, but very quickly passed to the Dukeries (Mansfield) Group and became 65E434 when based at the Riddings depot. Renumbered again in January 1957 to 5E534, it is pictured with dents and all in the premises of Darlington Forge in County Durham during 1958. Renumbered again in 1964 to KC2, it was disposed of by BRS in January 1966.

To a 15 year old Ben Ford, the night trunking Bristols of 1953 were his introduction to a life style that still loves travel. Ben's first experiences were with Les Iles, the foreman driver who was given custody of the prototype Bristol eight wheeler - 2F383 - running the night trunk between the Days Road depot at Bristol and London's Rotherithe New Road. It was in 1958 when Ben photographed OEL 293, stopped at a cafe at Sonning, just east of Reading. The Bristol eight wheeler was an HG6L, number 88.119, being first registered on December 1, 1953. It's first fleet number was 2F467 but received it's 5G247 numbering in 1957. Transferred to Bristol's Spring Street depot - when Day's Road closed - the eight wheeler came out of service in 1966.

8956 UG was one of 241 similar Bristol tractor units - model code HA6LL - that were supplied to BRS, 1D613 being first registered on January 10, 1961, before being allocated to Thornaby depot. On fleet it replaced 1D383, a Leyland Beaver wagon and trailer that had come to BRS from the nationalised concern of T.O.Harrison. As the Warrington based semi-trailer suggests, the Bristol was used on the overnight Queensferry trunk which meant drivers from these respective depots met up and interchanged trailers at Huddersfield. Pictured about 1962 at the Hownsgill stores at Templetown, Consett, the Bristol was to remain in service at Thornaby until it was sold on October 13, 1967. At it's peak, Thornaby employed about 120 drivers, 35 of which were on night trunk services.

Just like the Bristol had been one of the dedicated BRS tractor units at the start of the 1960s, the Guy Big J took over this slot in the middle and back end of that decade. Termed as having a 20 ton carrying capacity, the Rolls Royce and Cummins powered Big Js were bought in their hundreds for operations first at 30 tons gross and then at the 32 tons mark. GOA 457D came into service on September 6, 1966, at Bromford Lane, Birmingham where it was based all it's life. Regularly involved in hauling products for the motor industry, on it's second day of service it was delivering copper billets ex Liverpool into Yorkshire Imperial Metals at Leeds. It was to be recoded MF147 in September 1972 when Midlands BRS was created and the Guy was to end it's days on internal duties as a shunter.

Customer's liveried vehicles are and always have been, an important aspect of BRS/NFC operations. Registered in 1962, 784 CUM was one of about 12 similar Leyland Octopus' specially conceived to meet a testing requirement inside the Sheffield works of SPT. What looks like a conventional tipper is actually a side discharging bulker designed by BRS engineer David Waterhouse. The floor of the body is shaped like an inverted V so once the four sets of side doors are opened, the force of gravity allows the raw materials to pour out. At this point the eight wheeler would be about 150' off the ground having driven up a specially built ramp at the Temple Borough works to discharge directly into a furnace. Prior to this discharge design being conceived, it took a staff of about 150 men to double handle the materials from ground level into hoppers before being craned to the top of the furnace.

In the mid 1950s, Frank Butler and his son David were running about nine vehicles out of their Micklefield Road depot adjacent to the railway bridge in High Wycombe. 90% of their traffic was paper, hauled either for Hedleys or Ford's Blotting Paper, both from Loudwater. YKX 176 was only a couple of months old when pictured by Ben Ford in 1956 on the A4 in Wiltshire not far from the Ridgeway Cafe. Driver George Priest is hauling about 10 tons of waste paper from St Anne's Board Mills in Bristol back to Loudwater. Coupled to a Scammell semi-trailer, the four cylinder 287 engined Albion Chieftan FT111 with coachbuilt cab was recalled as being rather underpowered for this weight.

Driver Fred Rackstraw had just got this Leyland Comet new when Ben Ford pictured it in 1957 enroute from High Wycombe to Nottingham with 12 ton of paper on board. Going into articulation in the mid 1950s was a big change for Butlers who up until then had relied on the following rigids: NBH 772 - Leyland Hippo; SBH 453 and UPP 305 - bonneted Leyland Comets; OKX 486 and VBH 179 - S type Bedfords; AHH 126 - petrol engined Leyland Cub; PBH 443 - O type Bedford; TJ 3197 - petrol engined Leyland Beaver.

Bert Barber and Ernie Brooks were the two men behind the company of Canley Car Deliveries which was based on the Coventry by pass, about a mile from the Triumph works. CCD grew to around the 20 mark before being bought out by the James Delivery Service - who in turn were taken over by Tolemans. 4578 VC was one of their well liked

Leyland Super Comets that would hardly be tested with it's load of Triumph Spitfires. The outfit is a Carter built Carveyor which incorporated an electric lift to raise/lower the individual vehicles between decks. In this fully loaded position, the lift is in the raised position supporting the third sports car on the Leyland's top deck.

Top heavy haulage driver at Siddle Cooks was to be Walter Tomlinson but of all the towns he drove through in his 20 years at Cooks, Congleton is the one that really sticks in his mind. But I suppose when you have 60 ton columns like this in tow then it's more than understandable that progress in pre-motorway days was only slow. Destined for Ellesmere Port, the Redheugh construction should have gone by rail but a strike forced the change to Cooks. Walter and his team of mates - Gwyn Edwards, Billy Collinson and Joe Young - spent three weeks criss crossing northern England before reaching Merseyside. The only bonus to the the job was that Walter convinced Siddle to buy new boots for all the mates as he said they'd done that much walking, they'd worn their originals out.

One of the most distinctive looking four wheeled Scammells ran by Cooks must have been 4100 PT. Having a Mountaineer style cab, the 4x2 was built for South America as regular driver Ronnie Atkinson recalls finding a plate inside the cab relating to the Buenos Aires dealership of AJ Prudence. Converted from left to right hand drive by the Cook foreman fitter Larry Wilson, the Leyland 680 powered unit was quite a flyer with a top speed capability of 50mph. Ronnie moved one load of 60 tons and numerous 40 ton rolls from Glasgow to South Wales even though the Scammell was light on springs and stopping power. Accompanied by mate John Brown, Ronnie spent 18 months of his life hauling 70' long piling bars from the Cargo Fleet Teesside works to Aultbea in north west Scotland. Doing three trips a fortnight at 32 tons gross it was hard work just to reach Inverness but Ronnie still shudders at the thought of those single track roads he had to work out to the west coast.

Seen reversing onto the 'Isle of Gigha' at Largs in 8700 UP, driver Joe Devey had waited two days at this Scottish port for the sea to calm. Enroute from Vickers' Elswick works to Rothesay on the Isle of Bute, his Seer Drum incinerator load was one of several shipped out by Cooks to make the Western Isles self sufficient in rubbish disposal. Bob Suddes - head of the Cook installation gang - is stood beside the Cook made low loading trailer. The Billy Collinson look alike watching was actually a crew man off the ship as Jim Walton was the load's mate on this run. Whilst Joe Devey is still driving at Elddis Transport, the Scammell Highwayman ended it's days at Rush Green Motors at Hitchin.

Cooks didn't run many Dodges and Alan Hopps recalled his Perkins powered 4x2 FUP 300C had an insatiable thirst for oil, even when new. Alan is seen leaving the Whessoe works at Darlington on July 6, 1965, for a short haul across to ICI Billingham where a new plant was being built by the Kellog Corporation. Freddie Vaughan is pictured behind with the Leyland Beaver CPT 100B, both outfits carrying similar 10 ton loads. Driver Hopps still recalls the problems of instability he suffered with this 40' BTC 4-in-line semi-trailer with the worst load he ever had to contend with being some Marchon made soapflakes that were stacked 14'6" high.

It was in the 1880s when William Henry Cowburn was active on the Manchester Stock Exchange as a merchant. In payment of a debt he took over a concern called Parkinsons but rather than continue to use what was a discredited name, he blended the first three letters of his own name into the first three letters of Parkinson, to create the title of Cowpar Chemicals Ltd. It wasn't too long however before he changed this title again and for more than a century, W.H.Cowburn & Cowpar was the banner that was traded under. Progressing from horses and carts, the company's first motorised load carriers were to include Halleys. TF 8812 dates from 1934 and was originally ran as a platform vehicle hauling a drawbar trailer. The Model ES3 was rated for 13.25 tons gross, it's engine producing 67bhp at 1200rpm. Halley were to go into liquidation in September 1935.

From Halley, Cowburn turned to Scammell artics and were to buy the marque consistently until 1965. MTJ 675 dates from May 1951, the outfit weighing in empty at less than 8.5 tons. The headboard sports probably the most famous initials ever seen up and down the road. With the Cowburn traffic being predominantly acid based, Cowburns used a chlorinated rubber form of paint to try and withstand damage from inadvertent splashes. The start of the 1950s was a period when nationalisation was in full swing but Cowburns were to miss out on this programme as tanker operators were specifically exempted. Although the fate of MTJ 675 is unknown, DTB 210 - a Cowburn Scammell artic tanker dating from 1937 - was saved for preservation and is currently owned by Roger Austin.

When maximum weights for artics were first raised from 24 tons to 32 tons gross in 1965, the practical implications of the early regulations meant five axle outfits had to be operated to take advantage of the full weight rise. Scammell were slow to produce a suitable three axled tractor unit so Cowburn bought five of these 6x2 Fodens. Powered by the 210bhp Foden two stroke engine, they were a lot quicker than the solid reliable Gardners. Cowburn actually became a Foden service agency and continued to favour the marque until the mid 1980s. By then the company had passed from W.H. to his son Arthur William and then to his two sons Brian and David before they sold out to the Hayes Group on their retirement.

Those that can recall the 1950s version of the Scotswood Bridge over the River Tyne at Newcastle will remember an ornate structure that was a total bar to any oversize loads. Heavy hauliers were thus obliged to claw up the fearsome climb between Swalwell and Whickham before the descent down Lobley Hill. Crook & Willington Carriers may have had great faith in the prowess of Harry Maggs at the helm of VPT 85 - accompanied by mate Harry Simpson on the running board - but the climb necessitated the assistance of Miller's Diamond T. The 802 Lima base machine being carried on the 80 ton low loader also belonged to Millers who are still very active in the open cast coal business.

Born in 1897, Rupert Charles set himself up in road transport during 1921, trading under the title of 'The Direct Transport' from the town of Gobowen, just north of Oswestry. He expanded using both Foden and Sentinel steamers but experiencing problems with drivers, he decided to sell up the three steamers and invest in a new wagon, just for himself. Rupert spent £1,849-5s for this Leyland Hippo TSW4/1715, the vehicle order - which is dated October 4, 1932 - recording the oil engine number as 109. For his money Rupert also received a spare wheel, a tyre inflator, a platform body measuring 24'x7'2" and a totally enclosed driver's cab. Seen in early 1933 fully loaded with grain, the Hippo is pictured outside Rupert's house on the old A5 Holyhead Road, Gobowen.

Croppers of Kendal can trace their history back just over 100 years although paper has been produced at Burneside - two miles north of Kendal - for almost 150 years. About half of the Cropper transport fleet of the early 1970s is seen in this Oliver Acland photograph. The figures from left to right are : George Kissock, George Sandham - the fleet engineer - Cyril Colston, Colin Veevers, George Swindlehirst, Billy Tyson, Matt Towell, Derek Harby, Derek Longworth and Frank Forrest. The motif on the vehicle's front paneling is a cropper pigeon although drivers of old will tend to note the sheer luxury of radiator muffs and radio aerials, real signs of an own account operation. All the Seddons are artic tractor units apart from LJM 756 which was a 6x2 Leyland engined flat which stayed on for extended service. It was to be sold to Hardman's of Bamber Bridge then converted into a four wheeler for recovery duties. It was seen in 1992 on the M6 services at Hilton Park.

Hauling grain in bulk for the Timmerson Tudor concern of Mountford Bridge, Shrewsbury became such a Direct speciality that Rupert traded in the Hippo and invested in this Leyland Beaver artic. The original price of UJ 3700 wasn't recorded but the outfit was so advanced that it made the pages of Motor Transport on August 11, 1934. The Carrimore semi-trailer had a frame of steel pressings with hollowed out cross bearers which helped keep the unladen weight of the combination down to a respectable 5ton 8cwt. Even though it was occasionally ran as a flat, the true joys of articulation were yet to be discovered and by 1938 the Beaver had gone in favour of a rigid, with it's trade in value being £500.

After a brief dalliance with Leylands, Direct Transport went back to buying Fodens in 1937, a marque that's still in favour with them 56 years on. The gleaming unregistered condition and backdrop are obvious indicators to a Foden taken factory photograph although the six wheeler - which was registered ANT 870 - was not to spend a great deal of time at Gobowen. On September 7, 1941, it was compulsorily bought by the government for £1,200 and shorn of it's special Foden built beer barrel carrying body. It eventually went to France with the military where it was spotted by the man who had been the driver's mate on it when it was with Direct.

Opposite: During war time years The Direct Transport's activities, like most other long distance hauliers - were co-ordinated via the Ministry of War Transport. However the hostilities didn't prevent the occasional line up photograph especially when the Foden News came to call in 1941. Left to right the well dressed mate/driver combinations are: Len Walsh and Carl Lloyd; Russell Wilson and Andrew Lewis then Johnny Williams and Jack Roberts. Hidden under the sheets of the two eight wheelers AUJ 460 and BUJ 177 are loads of margarine whilst the centre barrel carrier - AUX 121 - is actually a DG 5/7.5 four wheeler hauling a drawbar trailer. This four wheeler cost Direct £1,250 in late 1938 although the price was reduced by trading in their Leyland Beaver artic. The DG 6/15 eight wheelers were Gardner 6LW powered and although just having a four speed gearbox, did have the luxury of electric starters.

Rupert Charles is pictured at the Foden works in 1946 taking delivery of his first new eight wheeler for 8 years. Because of the war effort, Foden channeled virtually all their production into military vehicles although a batch of six wheelers were sold to certain licensed civillian hauliers. In the eight wheeler's cab is driver Jack Roberts, who because he lived close to a chapel in Gobowen, was always called Jack Chapel. The Direct fleet were nationalised and became BRS Unit E67 but the Charles-Chapel combination were to continue when Rupert restarted his fleet after de-nationalisation. Direct are currently based at Hengoed, two miles west of Gobowen with Rupert's son Dennis running a Foden based fleet of three.

Seven good wagons with seven good drivers at your service seven days a week is how Arthur Duckett captioned this line up photographed by Douglas Allen. From right to left the drivers are: Clifford Burridge, Graham Parsons, Jim David, Tony Barrett, John Robbins, Jimmy Richards and Arthur. The eighth figure is John F.Moon, a famous transport journalist of the 1960s. 'Alstone Princess' was Duckett's second Rowe which was apparently one of the last to be fitted with the Perkins 6.354 engine. Fourth from the left is 'Alstone Baroness', an ERF Chinese Six stood next to Duckett's famous Guy Invincible 'Alstone Countess'. The second Guy in line -'Alstone Empress' - is a 4x2 Warrior.

Maurice G.Rowe was to build about 120 Hillmasters with 414 CYD new into service during 1958 as Arthur Duckett's first brand new wagon. Having a price tag of £3,000, the Cornwall based manufacturer gave Duckett £1,000 for the trade in of his weathered bonneted Dodge tipper. 'Alstone Duchess' had the Leyland Comet 350 engine and mated to a six speed gearbox plus two speed axle, was capable of 85 mph. Fitted with a 16' wooden tipper body, the Rowe was easily capable of 10-11 ton loads. It shares the picture with driver Michael Simmons whose claim to fame was in how he got his wagon stuck inside a building. Being fully loaded he was able to drive in through the low entrance but once he'd tipped his load off, the vehicle had raised itself with the natural spring in the suspension. The slight change in height was enough for the tipping rams to foul the entrance door so in order to get out, Michael had the let the vehicle's tyres down.

Bought specifically for a new coal contract, 'Alstone Lady' was first ran on a double shift basis between the Midlands and the South West. Fitted with a York trailing axle, the two stroke powered Commer cost Duckett £2,000 when purchased new from Prices of Earl Shilton. Arthur chanced upon the work when he heard that some Devon schools were waiting for about a month to receive a delivery of coal. Duckett was able to slash that lead time to a couple of days for as Clifford Burridge left Somerset at midnight to run up and load, Arthur himself would complete the run and deliver the next night.

Pictured outside Arthur's house 'Alstone Hall', 414 OYA entered service in 1962 and with a price tag of £8,300 was believed at the time to be the most expensive eight wheeler that ERF had built. A large amount of aluminium had been used in the tipper body and sub frame of the vehicle which was regularly driven by Johnny Robins. Recalled for his sense of humour, Johnny loved to sound off his air horns which trumpted the tune of the Marseillaise. At first the ERF ran north carrying 18 tons of sugar beet to Kidderminster then back loaded with coal.The script written on the front nearside is translated into 'I want the right'. This is rather poignant to those who know the story of how Arthur 'stole' this vehicle back when it had been savagely re-possessed by an HP company.

Opposite: William Feather was an ex farmer who set up his haulage business at Colne in the mid 1920s. It was to be his sons - Ellis, William and Alan - who developed the business, the picture in 1934 illustrating a premium line up of Leylands and AECs. Fleet number 11 was a Leyland Bull - originally petrol powered but later converted to diesel - that hauled a Dyson drawbar trailer and was usually driven by Ellis Feather. Long serving driver Albert Smith drove the Leyland Cub - on the far right of the line - which sported a single tyred trailing third axle and was expected to handle loads of 10 tons. Feathers started their business by collecting cloth and yarn from places like Oldham and Rochdale for the mills in Colne but it was to be their services to the north east of England that really expanded operations. By 1947 Feathers were running about 50 vehicles and in that year they agreed voluntarily to sell out to the Road Haulage Executive - the organising body that formed British Road Services.

In the late 1940s, Feathers kept busy by running a fleet of coaches but in 1954 Alan Feather bought back their old garage - built in 1936 - and set up in haulage again. With him was a Mr Kent who had joined the company in the late 1930s after he had been the transport manager of the Liverpool concern Smith Christmas. Two AECs were F & Ks first vehicles but in 1954 this quartet of Guy Goliaths had been bought through TGB Motors of Clitheroe. All the Gardner 6LW powered vehicles were to haul drawbar trailers and whilst 660 was a four wheeler, the other three were six wheelers. 665 is loaded with steel plate from Darlington Rolling Mills, the north east activities being controlled through offices at Newcastle and Darlington whilst a third office was operated at Liverpool. Of the four, 660 had the longest life at F & K for it was to be converted for recovery duties. Alan Feather was to die in 1970 and the business was subsequently sold to J.C.Ashworth of Bradford.

With a fleet currently counted at 130 strong, Fergusons of Blyth are one of the largest hauliers in the north east of England. They have diversified into all manner of activities, these currently under the day to day control of Alan Ferguson. It was his grandfather Matt who started the business in 1926 by taking the unusual step of selling his house to finance the buying of his first wagon. Pictured in 1937, Matt is seen on the left of photograph with his first employee - driver Jimmy Gaff - in the centre and younger brother Bill Ferguson on the right. By then Matt's early carrier work had expanded the Chevrolet fleet to three. His base in Bath Lane - seen in backdrop - was to serve the company until 1976.

Eddie Ferguson was to take over the reins from his father Matt and steadily built up the company during the 1950s. As well as harbouring great ambitions for Ferguson to expand, Eddie was also a keen photographer. In recording the mid '50s fleet parked in the Bath Lane garage, Eddie doctored the print by implanting a duplicated section of vehicles to give the impression that Fergusons were running far more vehicles than they actually did. All the removal van bodies seen were built by the Ferguson drivers onto a mixture of chassis. Micky Machin can recall the Seddon van pictured in the foreground was first used by Fergusons moving slurry on the Blyth Power Station construction site. The nature of the sticking load meant that many's the time the Seddon tipper had to be rescued when it had almost toppled over backwards.

Like most haulage concerns of the era, Fergusons were to expand by buying up either one off vehicles or small fleets, specifically to gain their important carriers licences. Whilst many people bought ex British Road Services' vehicles in this fashion, Fergusons can rightly claim to have completely taken over BRS. However in their instance the initials stood for Bairds Road Services and they only ran two old Vulcans. Another company acquired by Fergusons was Thompsons of Blyth whose history stretched back to horse and cart removals. By 1961 the fleet only stood at three strong plus a hearse and a taxi. FT 7297 was one of that trio, it being pictured assisting Glossop's Scammell Pioneer road burner in the centre of Blyth.

It was to be the very localised nature of activities that saved Fergusons from nationalisation although by the early 1960s the company had gone in for longer distance and heavier weighted work. Pictured about 1964, Alan Fellows is seen reversing a Guy Warrior Light 8 - CNL 266B - back into the Bath Lane garage. The load of concrete building sections has come from Concrete Utilities at Cramlington, their premises recalled as being an earlier base for airships. This eight wheeler - recalled for it's skittery rear bogie characteristics - was part exchanged for an AEC Marshal, whilst Alan Fellows retired at Fergusons in 1993.

George T. Fraser spent his life savings of £250 to buy six horses and carts and establish himself in the fish haulage world during the early 1920s. By 1946 his son - George junior - had taken over the reins and by 1960 his Aberdeen based fleet was counted as 38 strong. The horses weren't totally phased out until 1953 but by 1962 Frasers ran about 20 of these Thames Traders on long distance work. Sandy Robertson is pictured at the wheel of RRS 642 in Commercial Quay, Aberdeen, having just returned from Grimsby with a back load of new herring boxes. Although Charles Alexanders were to dominate the Aberdeen fish traffic, Frasers were to work the east coast with towns like Scarborough and Filey being visited every day with fresh deliveries. The haulier reckoned the Trader was good for a 10 ton load although mechanics like Derek Freeland had to extend the length of the handbrake to increase it's braking efficiency.

URG 166 was one of three Atkinson six wheeled rigids operated by Frasers, this one having the Gardner 6LW engine to drive the David Brown gearbox. Sid Robertson usually drove the Atky with it's Gray & Adams box to the London market carrying either fish or meat. The Thermo King refrigeration unit was powered on the move by propane gas, the tanks above the cab being refilled after every trip. As required the box could be removed by using a gantry system and when fitted with dropsides, the six wheeler was used to haul sprats in bulk from either Inverness or Burghead across to Aberdeen for processing. Pictured in Commercial Quay outside the traffic office and garage, the company owner is seen in a white shirt under the Fraser sign.

Frasers had four of these short wheelbase Dodges that were used in the main for road maintenance work by the local council. Office Manager Alex McLeod took this photograph of driver George Meston's vehicle parked in Riverside Drive, Aberdeen, when new in 1963. Having the Perkins 6.354 engine, the Dodge was fitted with Edbro tipping gear. It was only occasionally that the tippers were used on fish work and that was when any excess had to be transported in bulk to the fish meal factory. Fraser didn't operate artics until 1967, the first one being a TS3 Commer. At their peak the family owned company ran 70 vehicles but due to failing health, George Fraser junior ceased trading about 1978.

Hewitts of Morpeth are one of the few transport concerns that can rightly claim to have traded for 100 years. Starting with a horse and cart in 1875, it wasn't until Thomas Hewitt returned from the Great War in 1918 and injected all his gratuity into the business however, that it really took off. Not everyone could handle 50' long beech trees like this and Hewitts adopted their Foden six ton wagon especially for the task. Registered NL 4369, chassis number 10752 was new in 1923 and is pictured just leaving the woods at Nether Whitton - six miles north of Morpeth - enroute to Minto's Kirkley sawmills near Ponteland. The four figures stood beside the Foden are - left to right - George Miller, Jack Hewitt, Tom Hewitt and Alfred Miller. Sat in the Foden is the mate James McMahon whilst the driver, Joseph Oselton, is stood beside the rear bogie - a wooden spoked solid tyred axle from a Halley. Timber purists will note how the securing chain has been tightend by means of a band stick tensioner which in turn is roped secure.

Hewitts traded under the name of R.T. & J. Hewitt, a title that went limited in 1935. The initials actually stood for Rachel, Thomas and John - mother and two sons - although Tom was to be the driving force and actually later bought out his mother & brother's interests to the business. This line up pictured in a Bedlington brick works about 1926 was to record the first hydraulically powered tipper to enter service at Hewitts. Jack Hewitt is the proud driver stood at the door of the Leyland NL 5487 with next in line being NL 7122, a 6 ton Foden tipper - chassis number 11216 which was new in April 1924. Whilst NL 8409 was also a Hewitt vehicle, the Morris Commercial 1 tonner on the right was simply an interloper.

Above: ETY 387C is a Leyland Beaver that Hewitts got new and is pictured in the premises of the Redheugh Iron & Steel Co at Dunston on Tyneside. Driver Harry Peverley is pictured with this second hand 80' crane girder that had come out of the Redheugh works and was destined for a sister company, Redheugh-Willey at Exeter. The Hewitt built trombone semi-trailer is using Boden running gear. The white posts on the load's extremities were simply markers put there to avoid any accidents whilst the outfit was parked in the works over the weekend but removed before the long haul started. This Leyland - Boden outfit was one of the three vehicles being ran in 1975 by Hewitts when it's interests were sold to Fergusons of Blyth - a company that driver Peverley currently works for.

Opposite above: Long time Leyland users, JR 1553 is recalled as being one of the finest vehicles on the road - in 1932. It shares the photograph with driver John Hewitt - always known as Jack - the outfit being seen in Hewitt's depot at Spring Gardens Garage, Morpeth. There's about 10 ton in this boiler that was removed by Hewitts from an abbatoir in Gateshead and was bound for a woollen mill at Warwick Bridge near Carlisle. Supporting the weight is the old Halley axle still running on solid tyres. The one drawback to this Leyland Beaver was the fuel consumption of it's petrol engine so due to this, it was sold in 1938.

Opposite below: Because of their diverse interests - mainly based on timber and heavy haulage - Hewitts were not to be caught up in the nationalisation net. FTY 261, which had a 30 ton capacity, was new into service on January 1, 1951. It was collected from Fodens of Sandbach by Tom's son Alec who was given half a day's instruction in how to operate the 12 speed gearbox when driven by a two stroke engine. Pictured about 1952, Alec is loaded with two deck sections made by Wright Anderson at Gateshead and taken, for some experimental purposes, to an aerodrome in Bedfordshire. Taking the weight is a Hewitt built pole semi-trailer which is based on ex military Freuhauf axles. About 1953, FTY 261 had a tipper body placed on it and was ran as a rigid. It was later converted into an eight wheeled flat - courtesy of a new chassis and an extra axle - but when sold to a quarry operator at Staindrop in County Durham, it was converted back to a tipper.

Although Hills of Botley are perhaps better known as heavy hauliers, the reasoning behind the continuity of 100 years in haulage is their farming and agricultural transport arm meant they weren't compulsorily bought up in the 1950s phase of nationalisation. GAA 311 wasn't however, one of their better vehicles as the petrol engined AEC was slow and expensive to run. Jack Hill paid £350 to Ted Steele of Datchet for the complete vehicle in the late 1940s, the chassis originally seeing service in the RAF. Harold Read was the regular driver of a vehicle that carried sheep and pigs as a double decker then horses and cattle on a single deck.

DRV 648 was a distinctive Dennis Horla tractor unit fitted with a Perkins P6 engine and bought new by Hills from Sparshatts of Portsmouth. The horsebox was built by Jennings of Reading and although the axle location suggests awkward manouvering of the outfit, it did travel well on the road. Nobby Sessions, Reg Goodfellow and Ernie Smart were regular drivers of this artic which had a quick release Scammell made automatic coupling to it's semi-trailer. To create extra utilisation, Hills used to back load the horsebox with sacks of grain and cattle feed from London and Avonmouth.

Soon after World War II, the Ministry of Agriculture insisted that all milk producing cattle had to be tested for tuberculosis. Once the farmer had a clean bill of health, he was known to have an 'attested herd'. The sign on the Sparshatt built semi-trailer is thus very significant although the small RHA badge underlines the efforts Jack Hill put into the Road Haulage Association. Seen in March 1952, PHX 395 is a petrol engined Bedford bought by Hills ex Ministry of Defence. Toby is the dog on a watching brief whilst driver's mate Len Page, who spent 38 years at Hills, is the figure at work.

Once denationalisation re-opened the transport vaults, Hills - like many others - built up their fleet with ex BRS purchases like KOA 978. In total Hills ran seven wagon and drags on tramping work all over the country. This Leyland Beaver dates from 1949 and was regularly driven by Gordon Prebble and Sid Cook. Hauling a Dyson drawbar trailer, the outfit is pictured in the Botley depot fully loaded with chocolate. The Beaver ended its days at Hills converted into a livestock transporter.

287 JME was one of two similar Fodens - the other one being ROT 972 - specially converted from eight wheelers by Foden's depot at Cowplain, Waterlooville, Hampshire for timber tractor work. Although being a bit over specified, Hills also used them for general haulage work - there being a load of cased aircraft parts enroute from Swindon to Portsmouth on board. Jim Purvis, with Charlie Knight as mate, normally drove the Gardner 6LW powered Foden which had a rear winch and drop anchors. Whilst the Foden was destined to be chopped into a four wheeled tractor unit, the Tasker six wheel trailer was stretched to 70' long specifically for aircraft and hovercraft carriage.

In the early 1960s, Hills of Botley were one of the few hauliers in the south that could offer farmers a complete farm removal service. Pictured on the far right is Percy Yates who was moving all his machinery and livestock from Upland Farm at Botley to East Horsley in Surrey. Left to right the Hill drivers are Gordon Alford, Len Samways and Brian Vear. DTP 112 - stood in front of EPM 528 - is a Dennis Pax which carries a special tubular steel framed cattle container box. Both the Seddons in shot had the Perkins P6 engine.

During 1951 it was recorded that Hills carried a total of 1,857 horses although the company were keen advocates of using artics for the traffic so that the tractor units could also be utilised for other purposes. Seen at Botley are a pair of brand new Jennings trailers, the one on the left built to carry five horses whilst the Seddon hauled trailer - with Walt Jacob in command - could accommodate six. Albion Chieftan PCC 368 sports an all steel cab made by Autolift of Bolton. In the main these cabs went for export as they were made to split in two - the break occurring just beneath the windscreen line.

Wednesday July 24, 1963, was not the happiest day in the Hill calendar as the residents of Andover weren't particularly happy when this outfit took up over long residence. Enroute from Ludgershall to Tilbury, the 65 ton of Conqueror battle tank, supported on a Rogers trailer, came to a premature stop when the tractor pulling it broke down. Bill Miles was the driver of the Thornycroft Antar XMT 586 which expired as it was negotiating the Andover railway crossing. Jim Purvis was sent out hot foot in the Scammell Junior Constructor 874 AUU in order to drag the outfit clear of the lines although clearing the town took a bit longer.

60

Above: In the early 1960s, Sunter's Rotinoff Atlantic was one of the most powerful tractors in the land but even with their famous Foden 100 tonner as pusher, the 300 ton gross outfit couldn't negotiate the Hythe by-pass without the assistance of Hills. Enroute to Fawley, the Head Wrightson load needed the help of Jack Collins driving TOT 297 to clear the steepest stretch on the A326. The hard worked Scammell Explorer was cut up for scrap by Hills in 1972.

Opposite: Pictured near Tiphook, enroute from Croydon to Portsmouth, Hills' Queen Mary semi-trailer is seen making easy work of a complete Air Speed Oxford. The aircraft was road hauled west for preservation purposes and was in the capable hands of driver Jim Purvis. At the time of writing Jim had spent 45 years working for Hills whilst his current work is spent on welding and trailer repairs.

Many drivers of old will recognise this location as being outside Bibbys of Liverpool as the cast iron pipes on the wall were regularly known to crack open and shower the uninitiated. The Johnston artic is waiting to unload it's consignment of Marchon made soapflakes from Whitehaven, a pulley system being operated to reach the building's upper floors. In total there were four Johnston brothers, but whilst Jimmy and Tommy ran affairs, Jack was a driver and Hector had his own vehicle, albeit in Johnston's colours. Roy 'Indiana' Jones - who now drives for A.D.Boyes - recalls this ERF outfit had awful brakes. The 27' Northern semi-trailer is recalled as a Johnston special in that it was the longest trailer able to get into the Milk Marketing Board's Barrow depot to collect a load of cheese.

Opposite: After learning his haulage craft at Siddle C.Cooks, Alan Hopps set up on his own account in 1971 paying £5,700 for this new Scania 110 tractor unit. He also paid £1,500 for a new Boden semi-trailer, but it was only when he got this second hand King bogie from Rush Green Motors at Hitchin, that a lot of long load work came his way. There was about 42 ton in this pair of Wright Anderson bridge girders - both 130' long - that John Hopps is steering down Hawks Road in Gateshead. Driver is Cliffy Herbert who took over the Scania when Alan got his second wagon - an ERF tractor unit NTY 893F. Cliffy did about 10 of these loads which were to form the flyover across the rail marshalling yards on Newcastle's Western by pass. A second Scania - PUP 901M - was to follow but ill health forced Hopps out of business in 1977.

Below: As well as being bought out during nationalisation, Jimmy Johnston also sold his 15 strong fleet to the newly started H & L Transport in the mid 1960s. He didn't stop trading however, as he was soon to re-equip with GAO 900D being one of three Mercedes artic tractor units bought new from Cawthorn & Sinclairs at Birtley. George Therwall was the regular driver of this unit, the other two going to George Hodgson and Sid Eaves. Although the Cummins powered D Series Ford rated at 28 tons gross was recalled as being exceptionally fast over the ground, George Scott - it's regular driver - had regular boiling problems as originally the Ford was fitted with the wrong radiator.

Longbridge Car Delivery Service is recalled as not enjoying the longest of existences. The firm started with a Land Rover hauling a Carter built drawbar trailer to deliver first one, then two new cars at a time. When they saw the sloper built for Avon Car Deliveries they spec'd one of their own. 4558 VP was to prove exceptionally light, albeit expensive, due to the high aluminium content in the build. The petrol engined Austin Loadstar is supporting two Wolseley 1500s with the very similar Riley 1.5 at the rear of the main deck. On the trailer is a Wolseley 6/99, an upmarket version of the well liked Austin Westminster. The outfit is seen outside the main Austin offices in Birmingham.

KHS 473 dates from 1956 and was photographed by Alec Fraser northbound on the A6 near Penrith enroute to Scotland when brand new. The 5,000 gallon general purpose tanker was apparently the only one that McKelvies ran out of their Paisley depot. Jimmy Armour, who lived in Barrhead, was the tanker's regular driver, it's main job being on contract work for Esso petroleum. The 600 powered eight wheeler normally delivered into Prestwick and Glasgow airports. The small cab roof mounted marker lights being required when the tanker unloaded directly into parked aircraft.

Opposite: Although heavy haulage is not now a McKelvie speciality, during the '50s and 60s they had rose to become Scotland's largest operator in this form of traffic. Eric Steel recalls that DGG 799 was one of two Foden 6x4s - both coming ex MoD - which were totally refurbished at Barrhead before entering service, the S18 cab belying it's true 1944 vintage. Jimmy Castles was the regular driver of this outfit which was good for 35-45 ton loadings. Pictured in Orbiston Street, Motherwell, the Crane semi-trailer is supporting a small transformer. Being fully rigged, it suggests the load was on a relatively short movement between Meadow and Dalzeil steel works. When finally scrapped, the Gardner engines and Foden gearboxes from these two tractors were sold across to Ireland.

Similar to most heavy hauliers of the era, McKelvies pressed into service some strange looking trailers. Believed to have come from a crane company in Park Street, Motherwell, these solid wheeled load carriers naturally proved ideal for this crane girder load. 'Baldy' Sexton is pictured behind the wheel of MHS 344, one of two identical 6x4 Fodens bought new by McKelvies. Having the eight cylinder Gardner engine, eight speed gearbox and two speed rear diffs, the tractor also sported what many people thought was the best heavy haulage crew cab available. Plenty room for the mates and suitcases, the only drawback to the rear compartment was that it got so hot, although this proved to be an ideal drying room for clothes and towels on a long trip. The tractor was to end it's days on internal work in Ravenscraig steel works whilst the trailers were used as transhipping benches in the Frood Street depot.

Sister to OHS 612, PHS 141 is recalled as being the star exhibit on the Foden stand of the 1959 Kelvin Hall Motor Show in Glasgow. Having the 6LX-150 Gardner engine coupled to a 12 speed gearbox and hi-low hubs, the Alex Conaboy driven tractor gave many good years to McKelvies. Seen in Dalmarnock Road, Glasgow, with MHS 159 pushing, the photograph shows a girder trailer built to Jim McKelvie's own specification in the Barrhead workshop. Rather strangely it sports a short SMT bogie under the front neck and a four row Scheuerle bogie at the rear of the trailer. Road foreman Jock Lockart is pictured in front of the leading tractor whilst Jimmy Howitt is the mate at the rear bogie which is being steered by the unseen Peter Boyes. PHS 141 was also to end it's days on internal work at Daziel steel works.

August 18, 1963, saw McKelvies move the first of 12 similar gas storage tanks built by Motherwell Bridge Engineering which measured 130' long, 13'6" diameter and weighed 140 tons in weight. Seen going north towards Newhouse at Motherwell Cross, the load is the first of four enroute to Provan gas works - the others going to Granton and Kilmarnock. Peter Morrow is driving PHS 141 with his brother Jock, being the mate at the rear of the tractor. Peter Reilly is the travelling engineer sitting on the rear trailer which is again being steered by the unseen Peter Boyes. The car in shot is a Ford Classic which was owned by Willie Christie who was a steersman at McKelvies at the time.

In order to safely negotiate 'Jacks Brae' - a 1 in 12 climb in Motherwell - McKelvies hooked up three of their big tractors. The combination of 500 horsepower was also needed at the Cleek Him Inn hill between Motherwell and Newarthill, a long pull which could cause problems on a wet day. The 16 mile journey was to take the load 12 hours to negotiate. Carrying the weight is a pair of Scheuerle bogies that were running on solid tyres. McKelvies carried two sets of tyres for these bogies - pneumatics and solids - which permitted either higher running speeds or higher loadings respectively. Whilst these huge storage tanks heralded the start of cheap gas for Scotland, the passage of time was to see them made redundant with the Provan and Kilmarnock vessels being sold across to Ireland.

E.Patterson may have been the name on the door but it was his sons Ted, Harry and Alan who ran the Blackhill transport concern in north west Durham, predominantly of Bedford tippers. VY 8151 was their sole six wheeled flat which had been bought at least third hand from Parky Bates, the Iveston cattle haulier. The regular driver of this DG Foden was Stan Gibson, a man recalled for his total reliability and his love of cigarettes. Pictured here loaded with Consett Iron Company steel plate about 1959, the Foden usually carried blooms to Parkgate, Rotherham, back loading with bricks. Pattersons sold out to Salkeld Brothers about 1965.

July 4, 1958, sees Sheffield based Eric Morton about to leave Brush Electric at Loughborough with one of the many 90 ton transformers that he hauled, this one bound for Acton Sub Station. Eric went to Pickfords' Park Royal HQ to collect this Rolls Royce powered Constructor when new on June 21, 1957. Whilst M1662 was at the time an example of the latest big Scammell, the Crane girder frame trailer was by then a bit dated. Although it incorporated hydraulic suspension, each bogie had to be physically jacked by hand. Eric will tell you that it took 100 pumps of the jack handle to raise one end of the trailer by one inch. Thankfully however, it wasn't long before Pickfords fitted donkey engines to these trailers to take over this raising and lowering exercise. Harry Chambers is the steersman at the back of the trailer whilst Bill Fisher was the outfit's mate.

Above: Whilst modern day high capacity mobile craneage is almost taken for granted, in 1950 the Tyne's floating crane Titan II was something rather special. With another Diamond T - HOX 493 - pushing, GLU 654 is literally dwarfed by it's superstructure. This CA Parsons photograph shows one of their 140 ton generators enroute from Heaton to Toronto the weight being supported on T3440, a Crane solid tyred trailer nicknamed 'The Abortion'. Into service with Pickfords in 1946, GLU 654 bore chassis number 9800670 and was ran by this heavy haulier until 1962. Believed to be the only ex Pickfords Diamond T to have stood the passage of time, this tractor was saved for preservation by Tony Graves of Kent who has restored it back into it's 1950s livery.

Opposite above: It became a Pickfords trade mark of being able to provide bags of fire power - usually Scammell sourced - although anyone would find the terrain between Rosyth and Dunfermline particularly demanding when grossing about 300 tons. SUU 263 heads up TGJ 681 enroute to Kincardine Power Station although not forgotten is the pushing Scammell 80 tonner DUS 951. This Pioneer derivative started life with the Issac Barrie concern in 1947 and was to be used by Pickfords until March 1959. Pulling trailer TM413, the two 6x6 Constructors bore chassis numbers 9329 and 9602 respectively, they being worked by Pickfords from 1956 until 1968.

Opposite below: In his time, Eric Morton became top driver at Pickfords' Sheffield depot and although his Albion 900 powered Super Constructor did a fine job, the Pickfords organisation thought more of TM870 - the pair of four axled bogies that Eric hauled for 14 years. Coupled together as an eight axled load carrier with a 160 ton capacity, 870 is pictured on April 30, 1967, supporting a 100 ton casting that Eric had collected the previous day in Amsterdam. Destined for Davey United at Sheffield, the outfit has just left the 'Tor Hollandia' at Immingham. Whilst mate Harry Food is seen checking the load, the Sheffield manager, Ted Fitzpatrick, is the figure on the right. This was to be the last continental run that Eric did with this 6x6 Scammell as the following week he was to get a brand new Contractor, PGO 712E. It was a bigger jerk for Eric in April 1976 when he saw off his beloved TM870 when it was sold out to Fiji to deliver the 140 ton engine it was carrying.

Opposite: At the start of the 1960s, this huge outfit was to be the flagship of the entire Pickfords Heavy Haulage fleet. Birmingham based George Godden drove the leading Super Constructor whilst Harold Brown is the driver of the pushing tractor, WYH 902. The Arthur Philipson photograph shows the outfit enroute from Sheffield to Consett in April 1960 when the tractors were hardly three weeks old. Due to an all up weight of close to 360 tons, the roll housing load had a torturous route via Leadgate and Medomsley Edge before entering the famous steel town. Taking the weight is TM413, a six axled Crane trailer that hit the headlines in 1953 when it was launched as the first girder outfit capable of carrying 200 tons. Like WYH 902 - which is now owned by Gilbert Guest - this trailer has been saved for preservation and Ted Gowin was to put it through it's paces in 1992 at the rather wet Dorset Steam Fair.

Above: Pictured outside English Electric at Rugby and loaded for Edinburgh, VLH 427G was one of the many crew cab 125 ton Scammell Contractors ran by Pickfords it being new into service during January 1969. Originally based at Leicester, it was to be the fact that the vehicle was transferred to BRS Recovery at Newport that saved it from the scrap heap. Rob Willson of Goytre near Pontypool was to subsequently buy the Cummins 250 powered 6x4 in May 1988 and as well as restoring it back into it's original colours, he's also rallied it all over the country. With an unladen weight of 18.5 tons, chassis number WHV 4133 only returns about 5 mpg.

In 1882, William and Frederick Powell moved across to Tyneside, from Wigton in Cumberland, to start up a milk delivery business. They expanded this into the City Sauce & Pickle Co with their fine produce being delivered - by horse and cart - to all parts of the north east. The Powell's first motorised load carriers were a Lacre, then a Gladiator and thirdly to this Arrol-Johnston, pictured in 1907. Tom Tickle is the Edinburgh born driver who was brought down to England specifically to drive this Scottish built chain drive wagon. Stood at the front is the 16 year old wagon lad Jim Wilkinson but why his sister in law - Charlotte Titler - is sat on the crates of sauce isn't known.

It was estimated that Commer Cars built 3,000 of their chain drive RC models mainly for the military during the 1914-18 conflict. A lot of these were to subsequently flood onto the civillian market and Powells used their example until 1932. BB 2033 is seen in 1924 with Jim Wilkinson - now promoted to driver - on the right accompanied by wagon lad Tommy Fryer, with a load of jam in North Shields. The petrol engined three tonner is recalled as having a Linley pre-select gear change mechanism which was mounted on the steering column.

Powells took delivery of their first Halley - CN 3319 - in 1928 and paid £825 for the chassis - a £75 reduction to the list price for an identical new vehicle eight years earlier. Jim Wilkinson is pictured in Bewick Road, Gateshead, having just delivered to the local Thompson Red Stamp Stores. He's accompanied by his three year old son - Jim junior - who was destined to follow him onto the Powell driving staff. By the late '20s Powells were delivering as far afield as Glasgow and Sheffield. The Halley sports the latest idea of advertising headboards, the glass made structure incorporating a system of light reflective tubes in the shape of the Powell name. It wasn't set to last very long however, as the first severe rail level crossing encountered by the Halley shook the glass fixture from it's mounting and smashed the sign to pieces.

When the Halley came to Powells in 1928 it was painted blue and yellow, it being ran in those colours until 1932 when it was repainted to Powell's green. It is pictured alongside CN 3864 - a 30cwt Morris Commercial - that had just been taken into service to replace the chain drive Commer RC. Alec Watson was the regular driver of the Morris which tended to do north east work, only going as far south as Scarborough and Driffield. The Morris was ran until a stub axle snapped at Monkseaton and it wasn't felt to be viable to repair so it was replaced by a second hand Model A Ford - VK 3576. The Halley - which sports it's new wooden headboard - was eventually converted to pneumatics before being sold to a showman in 1939.

After trying Ford, Commer and Dodge, Powells bought their first Albion - CN 7458 - in 1936. The marque was to do the company proud and they began buying them regularly. CN 8669 came in 1938 and JBB 894 in 1940 but it was to be eight years later before LVK 417 came into service. Sister to LVK 416 - which came into service four days later on January 27, 1948 - the vehicle was given new to Jim Wilkinson junior who had just returned from doing war time service in the Far East. Sharp eyes will spot the aerial for the Pye radio fitted to the wagon and Jim paid £5 to have the hub caps chromed. The petrol engined six tonner is seen loaded with 700 dozen tins of mincemeat - in half dozen parcels - destined for delivery up to Glasgow. Chassis number 70650D did service at the Portadown factory between 1951 and 1956 before being sold to Blakes of Newcastle.

During the 1930s Powells began exporting their jars of produce - suitably packed in tea chests - to Ireland, the shipping taking place via Newcastle Quay. Their growing popularity encouraged Powells to branch out and factories were to be opened in Dublin, Portadown and Glasgow. ZD 8026 was a Dublin based Morris Commercial five tonner being new in 1947 and is pictured with a load of parcelled sauce. In the late 1940s, because of the shortage of sugar in England, Dublin made all the Powell table jellies and these were imported back to England via Liverpool. Although the Powell organisation closed down about 1969, the Portadown factory continued to trade but under the name of Goldenlea Preserves.

This Austin K4 - IB 9718 - was Powells sole Glasgow based vehicle and it's pictured in 1948 on the A74 at Beattock meeting up with the south bound LVK 417 and 418. The two Albion drivers - Jim and Stan Wilkinson - were using the round trip between Low Fell and Glasgow as an unofficial economy run. Both were attempting to do the 305 miles on a single tank - 25 gallons - of petrol. Carrying a full load of christmas puddings and mincemeat north, they ran back carrying a load of empties and whilst Jim was able to make the trip, Stan ran out of fuel just a few miles short of the depot. 'Big Jimmy' is the Austin driver seen on the left with Stan Wilkinson, Billy Curry and Matty Lowdon. The K4 was subsequently replaced by an Albion - NTN 676 - but because of Jimmy's love of Austins, the company bought him a Loadstar - OVK 487 - and the Albion was sent to Portadown.

Richards & Osborne can trace their haulage roots back through four generations to the company founder Captain Mark Richards. In the early 1900s he was to go into partnership with Richard Osborne and although this joint venture wasn't to last, the R & O title has always been used by the Richards' descendants. Based at Goss Moor Garage just north of Fraddon on the A30 in Cornwall, it's not surprising the company supported the efforts of another high profile Cornishman - Maurice Rowe - in buying some of his vehicles. A rare line up of six Rowe Hillmasters shares the photograph with several members of staff. Left to right they are: Forster Martin, Sidney Stocks, Keith Grigg, mechanic Darrell May, Henry Stocks, the boss Peter Richards and Morley Richards. Whilst the first four Rowes had Leyland Comet engines (the fourth in line is 472 ARL), the far two four wheelers - XAF 126 and XCV 248 - were fitted with Meadows engines.

Driver Henry Stocks recalls it was to be a red letter day in 1961 when he travelled up to Congleton in Cheshire to collect the brand new 302 XRL. Having just received it's Boalloy tipping body, the 68GX ERF was to be Henry's pride and joy for the next four years. With the Gardner 6LX-150 engine and David Brown six speed gearbox, the double drive 24 ton gross eight wheeler had a top speed of 38mph. Hauling china clay and china stone in bulk, it was later fitted with riser boards to carry sugar beet up to Kidderminster. At the end of it's working life, plans were made to convert the vehicle into a wrecker but these didn't materialise and the ERF was sold to NJ Grose for spares. Henry Stocks is due to retire in 1993 after 40 years service with the company.

Built in 1938 then into service in 1939, Ritchie's Sturdy ZE six tonner was one of only 55 Thornycrofts built with the Gardner 4LK engine and it sports a cab built by Northern Coachworks of Newcastle. During the war it regularly did two return trips a week to Southampton carrying wooden propellors for Short's Flying Boats. For two years it ran with a broken crankshaft - this only being spotted when the vehicle was overhauled in 1949. It then had the two ton of horsebox fitted especially for racing horse haulage. The vehicle, however, never lived up to the potential of it's cargo as it's top speed was only 30mph. Mechanic Alan Robinson on the left and driver 'Gentle Giant' Joe Wiseman are seen with the vehicle. Used daily until 1967, HBB 578 is still in Ritchie ownership and is a regular on the vintage rally circuit.

The Ritchie history can be traced back to 1898 when Ralph Ritchie used his engineering expertise to produce washing machine mangles and pedal cycles in the County Durham village of Hetton-le-Hole. It was to be his two sons Ernest & Norman who took the firm into road haulage and the fourth generation - brothers Stuart and Alastair Ritchie - still trade under this title. Although in their earlier days Ritchies ran a mixture of Maudslays and Thornycrofts, JPT 199 was one of two second hand Proctor seven tonners bought from Washington Chemicals that came into service about 1949 when two years old. Recalled for their Perkins P6 engine - which proved a swine to start - Moss gearbox and axles, the vehicles also had a speedometer which worked in the wrong direction - from right to left. Although these vehicles were scrapped in 1959, Ritchies still have a brand new Proctor speedometer in their stores.

As well as plentiful supplies of coal, the Hetton area of County Durham was also awash with sand & gravel deposits these being exploited by Ritchies via their subsidiary, Hetton Sand & Gravel Co Ltd. The brothers built their own washing plant in 1933 and it remained in use for nearly 40 years. Commer four wheelers were well liked for this area of work which saw deliveries into all parts of Tyneside, Wearside and northern Durham. The late Joe Bleanch is the figure behind the wheel of this QX model which was rated as a seven tonner. The six cylinder petrol engine never had it's cylinder head off in it's entire life with only plugs and points needing regular change. The vehicle was known to touch 60mph down the South Hetton road although naturally it's fuel consumption suffered at such a pace.

It became a Ritchie tradition that whenever a brand new vehicle was purchased, a family member would collect it from the factory and take the vehicle on it's first loaded run. Colin Ritchie is seen in the Spiller works at Newcastle during 1955 loading animal feed for delivery to George Wright's, the Hetton based feed merchant. George is actually pictured at the back of the Thornycroft Sturdy 6.5 tonner which was fitted with the similar Motor Panels cab that was used on the early '50s range of Guys. Sadly the vehicle didn't live up to it's stylish looks as it's hill climbing performance was extremely poor. Ritchie drivers said they used to switch off the vehicle's headlights every time they approached a hill as the Thornycroft used to die whenever it saw a steep incline. The vehicle was written off after it tangled with a Walker's steel artic at some traffic lights in Blackburn.

The Rooke family can trace their business links with the town of Tadcaster back to 1900. Timothy Rooke's two sons John Edmund and Charles Herbert progressed into diesel power although their involvement with agriculture and brewery work meant they missed out on the death knell of nationalisation. In the early 1950s they only ran a small fleet - which also included some tippers - PWU 716 coming into service during 1955. The big attraction in buying a 6x4 Albion Reiver was in it's high payload potential - a chassis weight for the six wheeler of under 4 tons. However the four cylinder engine only produced 93bhp and thus gave a modest performance. Fully loaded with 12 tons of barley, the vehicle shares the shot with Walter Derry who drove for Rookes from 1949 until 1982. Driver access to the Albion was eased by using sliding doors, the cab believed to have been made by Milnes of Leeds.

Vincent Rosleigh Salkeld - 'Bossy' - seen second from left and Victor Melvin Salkeld, pictured second from the right, were the two men behind the Salkeld Bros banner. They are stood in front of their two Foden eight wheeled flat flagships - 7601 PT and 640 PT - in August 1962. Sharing the photograph are - left to right - Bill Coyles, a Foden Salesman, Jimmy Hodgson and Frank Holgarth. The third S20 Foden in line is the two stroke powered 6600 PT, a 6x4 tipper that Colin Kendrick regularly drove, whilst the S18 Foden at the end is a four wheeled flat but also two stroke powered. JHH 800 came ex Robsons of Carlisle and although it left it's original 'Border Roamer' name behind, regular driver Jacky Goldsmith still followed a roaming itinerary with it. Jimmy and Jacky are still driving for the JSY concern based at nearby Delves Lane.

Although Salkelds favoured Foden heavyweights, VUP 597 was one of two - the other being 115 PT - Octopus eight wheelers bought brand new, together with several Comet four wheelers. Ralph Disbury got this Leyland - chassis number 570370 - new in 1957, it coming with a Bonallock light alloy body built onto the chassis by JS Robsons of Blackhill. The 600 powered eight wheeler adopted a dual purpose role in that although equipped as a tipper, it was an easy matter to drop the sides and remove the corner posts to carry general traffic including steel plate. Colin Settry in the centre and Joe Hall on the right are two driver's mates seen supervising the unloading of this 16 ton Leverton scraper box at Middlesbrough docks enroute from Birtley for export.

Marshall Eglan was the regular driver of 640 PT when it was ran as a flat carrying Consett steel but by November 1967 the S20 Foden had been chopped by Salkelds and converted for tipping duties. Apparently it was a fairly easy conversion to do, the removal of one of the multi piece prop shafts being the guide as to how much length had to be cut out of the chassis. Bossy Salkeld was keen to get into road re-alignment contracts and this Arthur Philipson photograph is taken on the A694 at Lintzford. Les Fairlamb is the operator of the 951 Traxcavator which had a 4 in 1 bucket as it could be used to load, grab, blade or back fill. Whilst the fate of 640 PT is unknown, it's sister 7601 PT has stood the passage of time with Freeway Haulage in Newcastle.

From their base beside the A68 at Rowley, Salkelds always ran a well turned out fleet, driver Kenny Goldsmith being entrusted with SUP 700E. Requesting 00 numbers from the Durham licensing office was part of their image, a practice copied from the famous Consett concern of Siddle C Cook. Salkelds adopted their red based livery from that of Redmires Sand & Gravel from Wolsingham and like this own account concern, strongly favoured Fodens. The brothers had a standing order to receive two eight wheeled tippers every year throughout the late 1960s with OPT 400D, UPT 900E, AUP 800F, WUP 600F and EUP 200G being all of similar short wheelbase build. Salkelds were to end their days about 1980 when they were absorbed into the JSY concern.

Ben Sayer is a name that's been part of the northern transport scene for more than 50 years. Ben himself began working for Frank Sharp of Orton being paid £4 a week to drive this International. Ben's daughter Mary Close recalls this load carrier arrived in Westmoreland in boxes of individual bits. The dropside body was built by Tom Stephenson, the Orton joiner who was also known as being the best source of butter during war time years. A regular destination for Ben and the International was delivering flagstones or chunks of granite from Shap to Scarborough. The only way Ben could surmount the fearsome Sutton bank was if he reversed up and that still took him 20 minutes.

Being a regular visitor to the Shap Granite works introduced Ben to Morrie Woofe and it was decided the pair of them should go into partnership hauling quarry produce. JM 3432 was their first jointly owned vehicle, the ERF being proudly emblazoned with their main customer's name although JM 5907 is seen here at Brough in August 1947, loaded with bagged grain. A regular haul for Ben was across to Teesside and the north east coast, back loading with cement from the ICI works at Billingham. The Sayer/Woofe partnership didn't last too long as Morrie began to develop his own Shap based garage and tipper fleet so Ben decided to go on his own.

Sayer eventually expanded his fleet to five with ERF four wheelers, the first six wheeled ERF being AJM 93. Driver Frank Golding photographed this line up during the mid 1950s, the respective registrations reading JM 7770, 7849, 6764 and 5907. Other drivers at the time were Les Rowlandson, Ken Dobson and Wyn Darque. Between loads the drivers were expected to help Ted Robinson build the Brough garage which is still in daily use. When Ben died in 1967 his daughter Mary took over the running of the business until it passed on to her nephew John Pattinson in 1976. John now runs a fleet of five Volvo tippers out of the same Brough depot.

These pages and the next two pages: The seventeen mile stretch of the A6 heading north from Kendal was, in it's day, probably the most arduous stretch of trunk road on the UK mainland. Virtually every lorry driver of old who ran up the west side would have his own story of the horrors of Shap. These Frank Scaife photographs were taken by Edith Wharton who lived in one of the cottages at Borrow Bridge, just before the final push to the summit. Taken during the 1930s, they illustrate some of the regular sights outside her front door - and even through the wall of the house. The six wheeled Foden in the dyke is Ralph Bullock's ELG 826 that Jim Coombes recalls always had horrendous brake problems. It later passed into BRS ownership and was converted into an eight wheeler. The official inspecting the Chevrolet through the wall is AA patrol man Arthur Jones who worked the Kendal-Shap beat on his motor cycle combination. Also of note is seeing Marston Road Services' famous Scammell 100 tonner, in ballast tractor form, pulling a rather light double deck tram. The two more modern shots were taken by Ben Ford and illustrate the highly popular Jungle Cafe - now the site of a caravan distributor - and the famous Leyland Clock, which is now preserved in the Kendal Arts centre. It is planned to erect a cairn on the top of Shap to pay tribute to the many drivers and vehicles who worked this stretch of road in war and peace, during all weathers, to keep the country's economy going.

From modest beginnings at Trafford Park, Manchester, when Ford first established themselves in the UK, Harold Colling followed Ford to Dagenham and expanded his concern to one of the biggest names in the car transporter business. This Carter built combination was one of only two similar outfits built specifically to shuttle vehicles between the factory and docks at Dagenham. Seen supporting five Ford Cortinas, it was the speed of loading/unloading which made the outfit ideal for this line of work. Harold Colling was to buy 23 Carveyors - wagon and drag transporters capable of carrying 9-11 cars - from Carters of Tamworth and paid £2,750 every Monday morning when he came to collect the latest outfit.

One of the early pioneers in long distance coal and coke work was Peter Slater whose Gildersome based interests were to eventually embrace over 100 vehicles. Peter apparently set up in haulage using the gratuity he received after he was demobbed following war time service in the Paratroop regiment. The money bought him a Bedford tipper which he ran from his home at West Ardsley, just north of Wakefield. With Ken Broadhead as his mate, Slater also hauled a drawbar trailer with the Bedford to increase capacity. However it was providing an unsurpassed delivery service during one horrendous winter that was to win Slater some long term contracts. To rapidly expand he invested in a batch of ex Shell vehicles - originally tankers - this 1949 AEC Monarch being sister to HYF 651 and KJJ 123. This four wheeler was fitted with a 7.7 litre engine whilst it's ACE built body was topped off with Slater made greedy boards.

Once established, Slater moved to a purpose built HQ beside the A62 at Branch End, Gildersome, next to Reg Gills garage. Another depot was opened at Penistone whilst the majority of Slaters tankers - which ran under the name of Bulk Liquid Transport Ltd - were based at Urmston near Manchester. NWR 745 dates from 1954, the four cylinder engined Chieftan being used mainly for coal work. This type of load was described as either singles, doubles or trebles - depending on the size of the individual pieces of coal - with the largest lumps being known as cobbles. Due to the seasonal nature of some of Slaters work, the company employed many part timers with some Wallace Arnold coach drivers regularly working the winters on the tippers. Some drivers couldn't stand the pace, however, and one of Slater's office managers reckoned that in their time, Slaters had employed more than 2,000 drivers.

It was to be the introduction of the eight wheeled tipper that really set Slaters up and although many Bradford tipper operators vowed it would never stand the pace, it was they who had to change to the Slater tune. NYG 382 was bought new from Oswald Tillotson in 1954 and because of it's registration, regular driver Geordie Fieldhouse was nicknamed 'Nig'. Geordie's 11.3 engined Mammoth Major regularly ran between New Market Colliery at Methley into Rochdale gas works doing three loads a day. The basic 1956 pay packet of a Slater eight wheeler man was £14 a week and for that he was expected to do two loads a day and one load on a Saturday morning. Doing a second load on a Saturday was worth another £1 whilst doing a third load on a weekday was worth a bonus of 10/- (50p).

OWR 88 also dates from 1954 and although it sports a Gardner badge, the engineer at Slaters - Bert Eastwood - reckoned it had an AEC 11.3 litre engine and gearbox. The vehicle was supplied by the Wakefield Atkinson dealership of Comberhill Motors who also fitted the lath type bodywork. 'Curly' was to be this Atkys first pilot although when he took over the job of Peter Slater's personal chauffeur, Freddie Harwood became it's long time driver. RWU 76 was another 11.3 engined Mammoth Major eight wheeler, it's regular driver being the diminutive Harry Brown or 'Don't say Brown say Hovis' as he was known. Engineer Eastwood will testify to the hard work that Harry put this AEC through as he had to re-line it's brakes virtually every month.

Although it was registered in 1950, KYW 16 is one of 1,700 Scammell Pioneer breakdown tractors built mainly for the military during the early 1940s. Bert Eastwood recalls the vehicle was fitted with a very good winch but progress to various parts of the country was always done at a very slow speed. Eastwood's mechanical prowess in his time at Slaters, was only matched by his huge strength. He was seen to be lifting eight wheeler springs unassisted - on their own a handful for two men - only one week after he had been rushed into hospital to have a ruptured appendix removed.

SWW 211 came straight to Gildersome after being exhibited in the 1956 Motor Show and was given new to Jeff Newton. Fitted with twin underfloor Telehoist tipping rams, Jeff really appreciated having the first vehicle on fleet with power steering. In the seven years that he had the Mammoth Major, Jeff clocked up 720,000 miles on the original 11.3 engine. Although it earned him many a bonus, Jeff recalls being fined £10 for doing 22mph - 2mph above his speed limit - on the Littleborough road after leaving Rochdale gas works. The Slater conceived crash bar across the front was later copied by many and was fitted originally to protect the AEC radiator. However, tales of haulage folk lore tell of Slater's vehicles 'playing trains' - pushing other vehicles in their path - and running over the infamous Woodhead pass at three abreast, when someone wouldn't get out their way.

In their time Slaters ran with two distinct liveries, the daunting black of old eventually giving way to a more friendly Slater green. SWW 850 is a 1957 Leyland Octopus bought specifically to haul coke into the Leyland Motors foundry. Slater was told in no uncertain terms that he wouldn't get the contract if the fuel was to be delivered by an AEC Mammoth Major - at the time one of Leyland's biggest rivals. Another Leyland in Slater service was a Beaver artic unit that hauled a 60' long semi-trailer that was built to carry railway lines from Workington to a Rotherham stockyard. A huge trailer in it's day, all sorts of problems were created for the artic's driver George Newalls. Telephoning into the office one day and being asked where he was, George said that the tractor was in Doncaster but the trailer was still stretched back to Bawtry.

Peter Slater was always on the look out for innovative ways to improve his service, UWY 473 being one of three specially equipped four wheelers used to deliver coal into out of the way places, too demanding for a tipper. The Charrold built body was also equipped with an extending arm which swung out a furthur 10-15 feet from the rear. Once activated, the hydraulically driven conveyor dropped the coal through a small hopper, which is seen on the AEC's spare wheel. In turn this channeled the coal onto a second belt which deposited the coal into the relevant boiler room or loading chute. The Mercury, driven from new by Bernard Gallagher, dates from 1958. In this year Peter Slater sold his Bulk Liquid Transport tankers to the John Ancliff concern who in turn were to pass into the Bulwark United Group.

Slaters ran two Atkinsons - one with a Gardner engine, the other with a Rolls Royce - which were fitted with semi-automatic gearboxes, their drivers being Joe Hall and George Mabbut. These two vehicles could be left in gear with the engine ticking over and they only moved off when the accelerator was pressed. Inching about under a loading hopper was thus made that much easier and Joe Hall used to just lean in through the cab door and touch the throttle with his hand. His dog Bimbo would normally sit on the driver's seat when this was going on so to the casual observer, it looked as though the dog was driving the Atky. XWT 775 dates from 1959, the year prior to Slater selling out to the Cawood Group although his name continued in use for some time.

Douglas Smith and Harrison Walton were the two men who founded the Smith and Walton concern in the mid 1920s and even though it's more than 30 years since they were taken over, the locals at Haltwistle still refer to the factory using this old name. Sentinel steamers were used at one time for deliveries but the fleet was to standardise on Dennis' supplied by Hodgsons of Benton Lane in Newcastle. Amongst the four wheeled Max's, ENL 93 - which dates from 1950 - was a six wheeled Jubilant whilst the company were to also run a Dennis Centuar artic. Although this had been a motor show exhibit, it wasn't a great success nor was the idea of putting drawbar trailers behind two of the Max four wheelers. A lack of power was the main problem as just getting out the works meant negotiating a 1 in 7 climb. The staff in shot are (right to left) Jake Strong, Jackie Archer, Les Bell, Billy Bushby, Jimmy Henderson, Hughie Haston and John Grant.

Like most own account operators worth their salt, Smith & Walton issued drivers with a smart overcoat and uniform cap as well as three pairs of overalls a year. Long serving driver Billy Bushby is pictured outside the main office reception at Haltwistle. With the Roman Wall running just a couple of miles north of the town, it's not surprising that the company adopted the Hadrian and Centurion titles as brand names. Rated as an eight tonner, the 1952 Dennis Max is loaded with gallon tins stacked three high. Having to hand ball all their load, the company drivers were adept enough to be able to pick up 6-8 tins a time.

When the Hodgson dealership changed their allegiance from Dennis to AEC, Smith and Walton invested in this pair of Mammoth Major six wheelers, the two dating from 1953. Whilst one was a 6x2, the other had a double drive bogie although in time both were to be converted into eight wheelers. Jimmy Henderson was the regular driver of FJR 774 whilst Maurice 'Crunchie' Smith was the normal driver of GHH 165. Maurice got that nickname because he always used to have crunchie bars in his bait bag. These two AECs normally ran south to make deliveries into the London area.

Painted in bright green with red chassis and wings, HTY 746 was a real head turner when it came to Haltwistle in 1955. Billy Bushby got the two stroke powered vehicle new, it tending to run no further than Smith & Walton's Newcastle depot or to make the numerous deliveries into various shipyards on Tyneside. When the Wallpaper Manufacturers Group bought out Smith & Walton around 1962, all the road going fleet was sold apart from this Foden and two small vans. The latter were used for distribution work, one into the north east each day whilst the other did deliveries around Carlisle and the north west. British Road Services were to take over the haulage once the fleet had been disposed of.

About 1964 the WPM Group were taken over themselves by Reed International and the decision was made to re-start a Smith & Walton distribution fleet with a quartet of AEC Mercurys. Billy Bushby drove BNL 979B whilst John Ferrol had DNL 729C, Maurice Smith had BTY 729B and Alan Burne drove DTY 436C. Fitted with the AV470 engine and six speed overdrive top gearbox, these 14 ton gross four wheelers lived up to their name with a top speed potential of 70 mph. Turn round was also speeded up when the paint tins were put first into cartons and then onto special pallets, three of which fitted the width of the vehicle. One of the Mercurys was later fitted with an ex National Benzole tank and ran between Darwen and Haltwistle on bulk deliveries. The transport fleet at Haltwistle was ended about 1987.

Brothers Bill and Albert Spiers established themselves in transport during 1931 and started off their haulage life with a second hand converted Chevrolet bus chassis - complete with wooden wheels - which they bought from the Witney Blanket Co for all of £45. The Spiers were to standardise on Albion four wheelers - BHW 916 dating from 1936 - and like most of the era were to slowly expand by buying up other peoples vehicles that were sometimes in questionable condition. Their main importance however was their attached carriers licences which could be transferred onto newer vehicles. The Ashley Albion was one such purchase although Rosina Ashley was actually the mother-in-law of Albert Spiers. The close connection of the two concerns is shown in how the vehicles share the same address and telephone numbers.

Fleet number three in the growing Spiers fleet was to be this 1934 Morris Commercial that was regularly driven by William Ashley - Bill Spiers father-in-law. Pictured in Spa Road, Melksham, the vehicle is carrying bags of chicken and duck's feathers for Sawtell's feather factory in Melksham. Spiers were to do a lot of local work for this company although it's premises were eventually sold in the 1980s to make way for a phase of house building.

Above: Pictured in 1949 with Jessie Simpson at the wheel, BMR 875 was by then 11 years old but was still being worked hard. Bought new by Spiers in September 1938, a record of mileages kept by the company revealed that in the six months ending March 31, 1948, the CX1N eight tonner had covered 18,164 miles. The BTC also felt the vehicle was in fairly good condition as in their valuation schedule they put the figure of £2,250 against this vehicle. Albion followers will note the distinctive profile of the rear axle, a shape still used when the Caladonian was produced in the late 1950s.

Opposite above: As a way of diversification, Spiers used four of these demountable containers for meat haulage generally up to Bath, but sometimes as far afield as Liverpool. With no form of refrigeration unit in use to cool the cargo, it meant for a non stop ride as fast as the driver could make it. WV 9828 was a K127 model Albion being fitted with a Gardner 4LK engine. Having an unladen weight of 2ton 18cwt 1qr, meant it was legally allowed to travel at 30mph as prior to 1957, vehicles over 3ton unladen were limited to a top speed of only 20mph. First registered in May 1936, the Albion was still in service in 1948 when it was to be valued at £1,500 by the British Transport Commission prior to nationalisation.

Opposite below: First registered at Sunderland in July 1935, GR 2016 was bought by Spiers in August 1937. Tipping the scales unladen at 4ton 10cwt 3qrs, the Gardner powered Albion M550 was rated then as an eight tonner. Not a lot of weight in these Stothert & Pitt machines but Spiers were paid for a capacity load when carrying them ie paid for carrying eight tons as for practical purposes the vehicle was full. Prior to nationalisation, Spiers worked a great deal for this Bath based machinery manufacturer.

Unless you were involved at the time, it's quite hard to imagine the devestating effect that nationalisation had on the hundreds of transport concerns that were bought up to create British Road Services. Virtually all of the drivers may still have had a job to go to albeit with a different employer, but to owners like Bill and Albert Spiers - on the far right of shot - things would never be the same again. This line up seen about 1949 of most of the fleet in the Spa Road depot would never be repeated. In BRS' eyes most of the Albions were probably overdue for the scrap heap although the strategic importance of the old Spiers depot was not underestimated because BRS still make use of it 44 years on.

After the Spiers brothers lost their transport company, they were to both go their separate ways. Albert went to Henley-on-Thames to set up a coach business whilst Bill stayed on to manage the BRS depot for a couple of years. Leaving this - as he enjoyed being his own boss - he bought up the Warminster Motor Co and ran it's garages until some of his old haulage customers asked him to go back into transport. KYD 209 was one of a pair of Vulcan vans ran on contract licence to Avon that hauled rubber soles and wellington boots from the Bridgend factory to the Northampton shoe and boot manufacturers. The vehicle, which dates from 1950, is recalled for the problems suffered by it's Perkins engine.

Opposite: CHR 380 was also bought new by Spiers and went into service during August 1939. The Gardner powered Albion CX1 was worked on the company's Manchester trunk, the canvas tilt type bodywork being required to protect it's regular load of Avon tyres. Percy Farr (pictured) and Bill Phillips were two of the eight tonner's regular drivers. Percy recalls this particular Albion had to be cosseted on a frosty night. If ever it was parked up for any length of time, a hurricane lamp had to be placed under the engine sump. If you didn't do that, there was now way the starting handle could be cranked to fire the engine into life.

Giving a far better performance on the Avon contract was this pair of AEC Mercurys which date from 1958. Used on the Manchester trunk, the vehicles carried tyres north then backloaded with fabric and chemicals from the Rochdale/Manchester/Liverpool area. To ensure the respective drivers always arrived home after their shift, the night trunkers swopped over at Kidderminster whilst day men shunted the vehicles at either end. Bill Spiers, on the left, shares the photograph with foreman fitter Eric 'Bodger' Dredge - centre - and Derek Shepherd who worked at Spiers until he retired in 1992.

Just like Albion had been a pre-nationalisation favourite of Spiers, the marque of AEC was to dominate the fleet line up in the company's second chapter of haulage. After 1962, Bill Spiers tended only to buy second hand vehicles, a custom that his son William still maintains. Pictured in 1971, the Mark V AEC Mammoth Major bears a Glamorgan registration dating from 1964. Seen in the company's current premises on Western Way, the eight wheeler's carrying a load of empty Dutrex chemical drums enroute from Avon Tyres to Shell's Stanlow plant in Cheshire.

Established in 1950 at an office in Wolverhampton, Starr Roadways got into haulage - like many at the time - by buying Special 'A' carriers licences and their respective vehicles when BRS and Pickfords were instructed to sell off some of their older stock. LBB 355 dates from 1947 and although it's registration suggests it started life on Tyneside, Starr bought it from Derby. Sid Smith was the regular driver of this 'O' type Bedford which is carrying a Ministry of Defence Hyster cable operated crane. Starr did a great deal of MoD work during the 1950s either on an inter depot basis or to their big sales point at Sudbury.

Most modern day plant people operate their own low loaders but in the late 1950s moving road rollers or Barbour Green spreading machines was still the domain of the specialist low loader operator. HUU 940 dates from 1947 and was another Special 'A' licence/vehicle bought ex Pickfords. The vehicle is pictured in Prosser Street, Bilston, the address that Starr moved to in 1955. They were to move to their current premises in Vulcan Road about 1959.

Even after denationalisation slowly allowed 'A' licences to come back into the private sector, long distance general haulage was still tightly controlled. More freedom was allowed in local distribution work - through 'B' licences - so Starr created a separate company, County Transport Services Ltd, specifically for this work. HOX 450 dates from 1948 and was one of about 10 similar 'O' type Bedford vans that worked within a 40 mile radius of Bilston. Their main traffic was foodstuffs that people like Quaker Oats and Nestle had brought to the Starr depot in bulk prior to being broken down into smaller orders for delivery.

Pictured outside the Foster, Yates & Thom factory in Blackburn, CKG 921B was enroute to the Midlands with this FYT made machine. The 6x4 Scammell Junior Constructor was the flagship of the late 1960s Starr fleet but rather strangely was bought by Anthony Hotham on the car park of the M5 Services at Strensham. He had arranged to meet it's owner there and along with Harry Littler - Starr's foreman fitter - he inspected and agreed a price for the Scammell on the spot. Coupled to a 60 ton capacity Dyson 4 in line semi-trailer, it was regularly driven by Phil Rider. Starr, however, found the Scammell to be too heavy for their class of operations and within a few years had sold it up into Scotland.

During the early 1950s, Starr had more than 10 dedicated sub contractors which displayed their allegiance through the headboard lettering. The Griffiths' Atkinson from Blackburn normally ran south carrying wool and Starr even employed shunter Harry Pearson to unload and load these subbie vehicles. Griffiths backloaded quite a lot of times with steel from John Thompsons - a large proportion of which went to Douneray in Northern Scotland. This weathered Atkinson was eventually replaced with a brand new Atky VTC 953, this latter eight wheeler also hauling a drawbar trailer.

Although FYK 970 - which dates from 1945 - had passed through Pickfords' hands, Starr bought the outfit from R & S Pye, a timber contractor of Elmswell in Suffolk after seeing it and it's licence advertised for sale in the trade press. These petrol engined Bedfords were expected to handle loads of 10 ton when ran in artic form but it was the outfit's hand operated winch that was often their most valuable asset.

Most of the Stevens fleet - but not all of it - squeezed onto Stokesley market square one Monday morning during 1964 within camera range of the famous Teesside photographer Dennis Wompra. The excess of men to machines is indicative of how some multi-axled bogie combinations ran with mates, long serving attendant Tommy Garbutt being seen on the extreme right. One noteable omission in the line up is Stevens' breakdown wagon, an ex army Scammell Pioneer that had been bought at the Ruddington sales. At a top speed of no more than 23 mph, travelling as far afield as Bristol to do a recovery took almost an eternity. The Scammell, however, has stood the passage of time as it passed into the preservation scene first with Tim Brown and then to Peter Waterworth.

Above: Stevens first multi-wheeled tractor units were a brace of ex WD Foden six wheelers, EVN 611 being the sister to EPY 901. Both were first registered in 1948 and both originally had the same DG cab although EPY is pictured in May 1959 in a much modified state. After tangling with a four wheeler belonging to Mowbray's of Boston near Leeds, the six wheeler's cab was extensively damaged prompting the fitment of a more modern S18 version. This was good news to Dennis Robinson one of it's regular drivers - although not the one involved in it's accident. Dennis had been one of the few drivers on the Stevens staff that was short enough to be able to squeeze his knees under the low mounted Foden steering wheel. During the rebuild, higher speed diffs were put in to lift the Foden's top speed up to a modest 30 mph and a conventional fifth wheel was adopted in place of the novel Stevens hook up hitch to the early pole trailers.

Opposite: In the annals of long length steel carriage, the name of Stevens from Great Ayton must rank amongst the highest. The company was well established when brothers Lawrence and Harold Foster bought it out in 1932 but it was to be Lawrence's son Peter (pictured) who expanded the modest tipping operations into long length specialists during the '50s and '60s. PPY 237 dates from 1957 and is recalled as one of their two Foden artic tractors that was fitted with the two stroke engine. Capable of a 45 mph top speed, such was the din from the engine it sounded as though it was doing 90 mph. The S20 tractor is coupled to a Stevens built semi-trailer hauling an awkward load of chopped steel plate.

Stevens early tippers and then artics had in general favoured the Bedford range first with O types. Bigger S types came like OAJ 638 which dates from 1956 although 1952 had seen the similar HVN 95 and HVN 232 come into service. Pictured on South Bank Road at North Ormesby, the Stevens convoy recalls an extremely busy period in their history. When a number of east coast towns like Mablethorpe were threatend with flooding, Stevens were given official dispensation to run literally night and day hauling Teesside made piling bars to the stricken area. The three axled Bedford artic also seems to be carrying it's fair share of weight as the three stacks of piles suggest a payload of about 15 ton. Whilst the Cargo Fleet works are now no more, it's distinctive main office pictured at the rear now forms the HQ of Langbaurgh District Council.

It was something of a Stevens speciality to run eight wheeled tipping chassis' as long length tractor units. Running normally with a Stevens built 4 in line independent bogie, 864 FAJ and sister Leyland Octopus 863 FAJ hauled all sorts of weights to all parts of the country. Dennis Robinson recalls that this eight wheeler only had the small Leyland 600 Power Plus engine which produced 150 bhp. But even that hauled 60 ton girders as back loads from Glasgow to Drax Power Station in Yorkshire. The climb out of Brough on the old A66 with that sort of weight was a real nail biter whilst stopping the eight wheeler at 75 tons gross could also be interesting as the second steer axle wasn't fitted with brakes.

AECs never featured strongly in the Stevens fleet with this Mandator and 947 FAJ - a 4x2 Mercury artic unit - being the only examples bought. Dennis Robinson is at the wheel of the 1964 vehicle which was only two weeks old when pictured outside the Golden Lion at Stokesley. The 11.3 engined tractor unit is coupled to a York tandem axled trailer which sports the luxury of landing legs. Prior to this, Dennis was used to hauling Stevens built semi-trailers that were leg free and when uncoupled had to be supported by a strategically placed oil drum. Dennis spent 28 years at Stevens and recalls the two years he had with this AEC were accident free apart from the time he was struck by a flying car wheel trim.

FPY 227D was one of the last Fodens bought by Stevens as by 1967 the company were buying their first of many Volvos. Pictured leaving the Malleable works at Stockton, the York semi-trailer is supporting 24" pipes that have been 'pickled' prior to dispatch. The pipes had been passed through a boiling mixture of coal tar to produce an enamelled effect before being wrapped in a tar impregnated cloth. The Malleable dates back to 1860 and when it's 42" pipe mill closed in 1970, it alone had made over a million tons or 6,250 miles of pipe. Stevens are still serving the north east steel industry with Peter's son John Foster currently running three Scania and three Volvo long length 38 tonne artics.

Philip Braithwaite carried all sorts of loads when he was driving LAJ 670 at Sunters but this American built Michigan ex WD 15 ton mobile crane is believed to have been a load sub contracted through Starr Roadways at Bilston during 1959. Sunters bought a batch of these 11.3 engined Mammoth Majors through the Oswald Tillotson dealership. Philip recalls the AEC was more than capable of taking 30-40 ton loads in it's stride and is seen coupled to an Alton made semi-trailer running on huge 16.00x20 tyres. The small hand winch on the trailer neck was regularly manhandled by Braithwaite as 40 ton railway locomotives hauled out of Ashmore Bensons on Teesside were expected to be self loaded by this back breaking winch power.

Pictured unloading in Lowestoft, HPY 53D is recalled as being Sunters only four wheeled Guy Invincible tractor unit that was powered by a Cummins engine, it being regularly driven by Eric Hancock. A far more common sight to the Sunter men of old were these loads of pipes being transported in their hundreds to all parts of the UK. Manufactured by the South Durham Iron & Steel Company's Malleable Works in differing sizes - these were 30" - they were supported in transit on wooden saddles and secured by conveyor belt style strapping supplied by the pipe manufacturer.

Go and visit the Cleveland Centre at Middlesbrough today and it's hard to imagine that Linthorpe Road used to carry all manner of traffic heading 'over the border' to Middlesbrough docks. This series of shots was taken by Dennis Wompra and show Sunter's Rotinoff bisecting the town in May 1968 with what was to be the first of five similar Whessoe vessels. At 95 ton in weight they hardly tested the 200 ton capacity Crane girder trailer although the four loads that followed were to be carried on Sunters solid bogies. This was because it afforded better access under the unloading sheer legs on Dent's Wharf. Whilst Peter Clemmett is driving the Rotinoff, the distinctive figure of John Robinson is seen on the offside running board. Harry Burn was driving the pushing 447 DPY with 'Old' George Wrightson as one of the mates, whilst the gesticulating form of Peter Sunter can also be seen in action.

February 27, 1975, saw TPY 675H crossing the Pennines near Sheffield with a locomotive used by Hitler during World War II. Enroute from Hull to the Railway Museum at Carnforth, this was reported as being the only loco that moved on this day due to a dispute by signalmen affecting the entire BR network. Even spread over eight rows of Nicolas running gear, a premature stop of the load was forced at Tintwistle to allow for some newly laid tarmac to harden. John Robinson - Sunter's finest heavy haulage driver - is the figure behind the wheel of a Scammell Contractor that was to be refurbished then re-registered YVN 308T. In the late 1980s it was repainted again before being sold out to India where even more hard work was ahead of it working for the Lift and Shift concern.

Swains of Poynton in north east Cheshire are a high profile company that currently run a premium fleet of 30 maximum weight artics but they can trace their roots back to grandfather Frederick Swain and his first Vulcan MB 7273. Fred's son Harry recalls that the new vehicle cost Swains about £400 in 1923 and was supplied by Johnnie Hibbet of Macclesfield. Sammy Wright was the vehicle's first driver although Ellis Bailey drove it for most of it's five year stay at Swains. The regular run for the Vulcan was taking churns of milk into Manchester and collecting feed from the British Oil & Cake Mills or the CWS Sun Mills for use on the Cheshire farm.

The Ward Brothers - Alan and Thomas - set up in transport in 1964 working out of Rookhope on the western side of County Durham. Although their first new wagon was an Albion, ERFs soon became a favourite and these three Metalair powder tankers were each to cover over 1.25 million miles. Most of this distance was spent running between the Weardale Lead Company and ICI Runcorn carrying flourspa. Although they have consecutive registration numbers, the prominent Edbro tipping rams under the 470 cu ft tank of 155H ran at 26 tons gross - two tons more than the two 450 cu ft tankers. Chester 'Chet' Robson, a long serving Ward driver, is the happy face on the left with Geoff Smith in the centre and George Holmes on the right. The latter two were Pontefract based drivers, the Yorkshire town where Wards operated a change over to keep these busy ERFs running. Ward Bros Transport is now under the control of Alan's son Angus.

The hamlet of Justicetown may be hard to find on the map, but lying within coasting distance of the A74, it's proved an ideal base for the north cumbrian owner/driver of R.D.Wardle. Christend Ronald Dickson, everyone has known him since schoolboy days by the name of Paul. He began his owner driving life with SHH 381, a vehicle he had driven since new for it's original owner, the ex Robsons driver Davey Coulthard. When Davey decided to give up transport, Paul bought the two stroke Commer and it's important 'A' licence from him for a total of £2,100. Paul clocked over a quarter of a million miles with the Commer before he traded it in for a new Maxiload. This and a third Commer bought some time later never proved as trouble free although PRM 282M - an 'A' series ERF four wheeler - was taken into service in 1974 and at the time of writing is still being worked by Paul.

James Watkinson began in transport back in 1925 using a horse and cart. Always based at Keighley, it was to be the woollen trade that was the company's main source of traffic until they began delivering the beams of John Smith's cranes. Whilst an ex BRS Maudslay Meritor eight wheeler registration number FET 871 was first used in conjunction with a bogie in a dual purpose role, SWR 602 was Watkinsons first real 'abnormal' outfit. The 1956 Leyland Hippo was bought second hand from the famous Keighley lathe manufacturer of Dean Smith & Grace who trace their history back to 1865. The six wheeled bogie, which is believed to be a cut down AEC Mammoth Major, came from Kingsbury Concrete. Cyril Rye was the regular driver of this outfit with Frank Toothill as his first mate, the combination hauling a large number of Wright Anderson fabrications from Keighley down to Hampshire. The Hippo ended it's days about 1965 when it was cannibalised into another Leyland four wheeled tractor.

AWR 490B is pictured outside John Smiths Cranes at Keighley supporting a 23 ton beam. Watkinsons bought this ERF because they couldn't get a similar Foden, quick enough. Although it's recalled as being a good enough vehicle, the 10 speed David Brown gearbox gave too high a gearing for the haulier's liking. The first driver of this 150 Gardner powered vehicle was Jim Howe, a native of Consett, who leant his craft with the timber concern of Tunnicliffes. 4609 WX is the third eight wheeler in line whilst the facing TSF 204 was bought second hand from Kelman's of Turriff.

Below: Seen in Clough Road, Hull, 4609 WX has just left the Kingston works with a load of arched beams for a new dye house in Batley. Keith Watkinson is at the wheel of this well liked Foden with Harold Smith being the mate stood on the nearside checking the outfit's alignment. The Crane tandem axled bogie was held in position by a pair of rails which were joined to the turntable mounted above the eight wheeler's double drive bogie. Of equal note is the width indicator mounted at the front of the S20 cab. As the canopy suggests, when not used on bogie work, the 150 Gardner powered vehicle was used for wool carriage. This Foden was to be later cut down and converted into a six wheeled artic tractor unit.

In the early 1960s, Watkinsons bought out the Pudsey based heavy haulier of William Lye although the name was retained in use for some time. The purchase was done specifically to get the heavy haulage licences although attached to them were three Leyland powered low loaders. JUA 853E was a replacement to one of these ageing Beavers and was believed to have been one of the first Deutzs in the UK. The air cooled V8 engined tractor was rated as a 30 tonner and given first to Jim Howe before Bob Raistrick became it's regular driver. The Walker semi-trailer being hauled came second hand from Seabourne Pan-European Transport Services and proved to be highly versatile. Although it flexed rather badly when 28 ton boilers were placed into the 30' long well, it's shape meant it was ideal to support the carriage of long steel up to 80' in length.

James Watkinson wasn't exactly pleased when his son Keith told him he'd just bought this 6 ton Hydrocon crane, in fact his first remark was that he should go and un-buy it. Keith was able to assure his father that the £2,500 investment in their first mobile crane was money well spent and after six months of some pre-arranged work, the vehicle had paid for itself. Harold Smith is the figure in shot, the Wright Anderson beam he's guiding destined for storage at Walls Shipping in Keighley. The 6 tonner was kept in use until replaced by a larger 10 ton capacity Hydrocon.

This outfit cost Watkinsons £3,000 when bought second hand from a plant hire company in Burnley. The Dyson 4 in line semi-trailer was rated as a 30 tonner although the natural inbuilt strength allowed it to haul a total of three 51 ton boilers from Glasgow. The tyres didn't really like such loadings and on one of these hauls, three of them blew out at Brough prompting a phone call to Sunters at Northallerton asking for some new rubber. Wilf Pawson was the regular driver of this 6x4 Atkinson which sported a 220 Cummins engine and ZF gearbox. The outfit is seen just leaving the Stone Manganese premises at Birkenhead.

After taking delivery of their first Scania-Vabis from the B & W dealership of Wolverhampton in 1967, Watkinsons soon became converts to the Scania marque. The 110 model was recalled as being a superb wagon, XYG 819G being pictured in reverse gear at Harwich with Brian Dale at the wheel. The haulier was to deliver these awkward Birkenhead made propellors to virtually every shipping country in Europe including one memorable haul to Sicily. There is about 25 ton in this load which is being carried on a tilt frame to reduce it's overall width.

When it came new to Keighley, MWX 940K was to be the Watkinson flagship. With 12 speed gearbox, two speed reduction hubs and an 8LW Gardner engine, this 6x4 Foden could do virtually anything. Pictured on 7th April 1972, the vehicle is hauling a crane girder made by Mattersons of Rochdale which was enrote to Eire via B & I's Swansea to Cork ferry. When compared to the Scanias however, the S40 cabed Foden was rather dated and even though it did a lot of concrete beam traffic out of Faircloughs of Accrington, it was never a driver's favourite. It was sold on at a fairly young age to R K Crisp, who were the transport arm of British Crane Hire.

As the motif on the front of these vehicles proclaim, it was to be the invention by a chemist called Fleming of so called 'elephant hide' that was to transform the paper manufacturing business of Ben, Sam and William Whiteley. Based at Pool, just outside Otley, the company felt BRS never took good enough care of their paper products so they preferred to run their own fleet and use certain local sub contractors like Peter Midgley. This line up in front of the '53 mill shows the entire fleet in 1958. NAK 171 dates from 1956 and being the newest Mammoth Major was given to George Milner, who was then the senior driver. JAK 602 dates from 1952 and it had Jack Carter in control whilst the four wheeled Monarch HKY 16, also of '52 vintage, was driven by the ex navy man Derek McCormack. UUA 417, the Ford Thames 4D or Costcutter as they were called, was usually driven by Jack Twine. The AECs were all supplied by Oswald Tillotsons with the eight wheelers having the 9.6 litre engines and double drive bogies. Up to 15 drops could be on the back of these vehicles, the paper being in great demand for insulation purposes in the heavy electrical industry. It was to be the advances of the plastic industry which was to cause Whiteleys to sell out about 1980.

Although now based at Waterlip - three miles west of Shepton Mallett - the company of Willmotts is normally linked to their first home of Wells. George Willmott ploughed his World War I army gratuity into buying a solid tyred Napier to set up in transport in 1919. George is pictured outside Wells post office, the Daimler three tonner dating from 1926. This vehicle was one of the last wagons built by the Coventry company before they went totally into bus production. The four litre petrol engined wagon was worked on the carrier route between Bristol and Street - via Wells and Glastonbury - which meant that Willmotts were licensed to deliver or collect virtually anything along that stretch of roadway.

1936 was an important year in the Willmott calendar for it was then they took delivery of their first brand new AEC Mammoth. CLJ 627 was petrol engined and is recalled as only doing 3 mpg with regular driver being Harry Curtis. Bert and Charlie were the two local carpenters who built the tilt body especially for cheese transport. Loading the cheese rounds could be a lengthy job. The body was wide enough to get six rounds across and then wooden boards were inserted so the soft 80 lbs cheeses were stacked four or five rows high. When not hauling traditional farm house Cheddar from Maiden Newton in Dorset up to Wells, the AEC ran up to Scotland for loads of Somerset bound cheese that had been brought ashore from the outer isles by rowing boat.

George Willmott - like many hauliers of the era - was to loose his entire road haulage fleet when it was compulsorily nationalised about 1949. He was then to run his own fleet of coaches but as soon as the politicians allowed, he began buying lorries again. AEC were strongly favoured but WYD 981 indicates that in 1956 you bought what ever was available. The Gardner engined Guy Invincible was recalled as being a lovely vehicle to drive but it was dreadfully slow. During the fuel shortage following the Suez crisis the company was encouraged to haul drawbar trailers to increase vehicle utilisation. Herby Lintle, who worked for Willmotts for 33 years, was the regular driver of this eight wheeler. It ended it's days at Willmotts being converted into a six wheeler for recovery duties before being exported.

The AEC Mammoth Major eight wheeled rigid was to be the Willmott flagship during the 1950s and early '60s. 912 KYB dates from 1961 and it's signifigance is that it was the last vehicle to have it's body built by Ralph Manship. Ralph was to join the company as it's carpenter but when George Willmott retired in 1960 to allow his two sons take control, Ralph was moved up to transport manager. When George died in 1965, Ralph was made a director as a reflection of the contribution he had made to Willmotts success. He was to contribute a furthur 24 years until his retirement in 1989 at the age of 70.

DYA 877C was one of the last Mark 5 AEC Mandators ran by Willmotts and is pictured about 1966 leaving the St Cuthbert's paper mill at Haybridge, just outside Wells. Driver is Ron Addie and he's carrying about 20 tons of paper destined for John Dickinson's at Hemel Hempstead - famous for their Basildon Bond writing paper. Of main note on the AEC is the word London indicating how in 1962 the brothers Willmott - Eric and Ralph - had opened up an office in Royal Mint Street, London E.1. Ran as a clearing house, the office also provided back loads for the capital bound Willmott vehicles until it was closed in 1975.

The Ergomatic AEC range was the standard Willmott work horse for nearly 20 years and the company were to buy five of the last six AEC Mandators that were built prior to the Southall works ceasing production. FYB 430C was actually a lighter AEC Mercury and was the first vehicle on fleet kitted out with a tilt cab. The clean lines of the well sheeted load on this Boden 33' semi-trailer hides a load of Babycham, the outfit pictured heading up Pensford Hill with Ray Welsh at the wheel. It was a similar load that nearly brought Ray to grief early one morning when he was climbing Doulting Hill and hit a patch of ice. Ray lost all traction and the only way the outfit wouldn't slide back was if the footbrake was held firmly on. Even though his leg swelled up immensely, Ray held the wagon until Manager Manship was called out to watch him reverse back to safety.

Being the first Diamond T to have a Meadows diesel inserted in place of the original Hercules engine, fleet number 234 went through a phase of poor reliability although it's pictured stationary here on the old A1 waiting for a police escort through the town of Darlington. Frank Leyton was the driver and he's enroute from Vickers at Barrow to one of the north east shipyards on the Tyne. There's only about 40 tons in the propellor but even carried at an angle, they were still an awkward load which needed great care. The weight is being supported on an early Wynns built tilt frame which only allowed for a few inches of angular movement. Note should be made as to how Frank is waiting on the wrong side of the road so that his overhang creates the least inconvenience to passing traffic.

Although Wynns never set themselves up originally as specialist heavy hauliers, it was to be this and other specialist aspects which assured their continuance after the late 1940s wave of nationalisation had taken most of their fleet. DDW 18 came into service in 1942 as one of only three Foden 100 ton specials. It gave the Welsh haulier almost 20 years of solid if somewhat slow service with Stan Philips being it's last regular driver. Pictured on Llantarnan Road, Leven, Newport, it's load is a slag reduction mobile crusher mounted on American design Athey crawler tracks. Normally fitted with a crawler forecarriage, the crusher has had this removed to ease transportation. Carrying the weight is what was known as the Rotinoff trailer which had an 18' long well but was tapered outwards to give an 11' width across the back bogie.

Wynns rose to heavy haulage fame due to some sterling service given by their sextet of modified M26 Pacific tank transporters. Originally fitted with 18.5 litre Hall Scott petrol engines, Wynns' staff refitted the tractors first with Hercules, then Meadows diesel engines before standardising on Cummins. In August 1958 'Helpmate' was yet to receive it's new Cummins power pack but it still found this 100 ton marine gearcase easily within it's capacity. Built by Vickers Armstrong at Barrow-in-Furness, the load was on a relatively short haul to the Barrow Buccleugh Dock. Running width of the outfit was almost 19' whilst it's travelling height was 23'.

One thing the strange design of the Diamond T gave to the heavy haulage profession was the space for mates to ride outside the cab but still be in a position to observe backwards and communicate with the driver. The 'Caution Extra Wide' boards were a standard fitment on these tractors of Wynns but one thing that didn't stay too long was the single red lamp that Wynns displayed to the front, adjacent to the offside corner as a sign of danger to other road users - the Police said they were illegal. ODW 937 is being driven by Rex Evans with Johnny Downs being the mate on the right. Resting on the Scheuerle trailer is 50 tons of boiler enroute from Wakefield. The 6x4 tractor sports one of the cabs specially built for Wynns by Nash & Morgan of Coleford in the Forest of Dean as a replacement to the rusting original.

The eight wheeler has always been a solid workhorse and to many, the Guy Invincible was a classic of it's time. TDW 991 dates from 1964 and is carrying a 12' wide propellor which is one of dozens transported by Wynns. Pictured on Cardiff Road outside Belle Vue Park at Newport, the Guy is also a reminder that Wynns were South Wales agents for this Wolverhampton based truck manufacturer.

Advances made in roll on/roll off shipping has meant that long distance haulage of exceptionally heavy loads is now kept to a minimum. However, when you have a train weight of 300 tons plus, even the shortest of moves can be testing when a 1 in 7 incline gets in your path. Wynns were forced to climb Barrack Hill in Newport in order to miss a low bridge when they were taking this 140 ton transformer into Uskmouth Power Station. It's easy to imagine the smell and the deafening Cummins roar as the outfit claws it's way ever upwards under the backward walking supervision of John Wynn.